THE USES OF THE UNIVERSITY

Fifth Edition

THE
USES
OF
THE
UNIVERSITY

CLARK KERR

HARVARD UNIVERSITY PRESS
Cambridge, Massachusetts
London, England

The Godkin Lectures on the Essentials of
Free Government and the Duties of the Citizen
were established at Harvard University in 1903
in memory of Edwin Lawrence Godkin (1831–1902).
They are given annually under the auspices of the
Harvard Graduate School of Public Administration,
which in 1966 was renamed the John F. Kennedy
School of Government.

Library of Congress Cataloging-in-Publication Data
Kerr, Clark, 1911–
The uses of the university / Clark Kerr.—5th ed.
p. cm.
"The Godkin lectures on the essentials of free government
and the duties of the citizen"—T.p. verso.
Includes bibliographical references and index.
ISBN 0-674-00532-5
1. Education, Higher. I. Title.

LB2325 .K43 2001
378—dc21   00-053942

CONTENTS

A New Century for Higher Education

I wrote in my Godkin Lectures at Harvard in 1963 that "universities in America are at a hinge of history: while connected with their past, they are swinging in another direction." I thought I knew the direction in which they were then swinging, and history has proved that I was generally correct. I was then looking as far ahead as the end of the twentieth century.

Now we have entered the twenty-first century, and once again I see universities in America at a hinge of history. This time, however, I see the hinge flapping in the winds blowing from many directions—no zephyrs, alas. So I have added a new chapter reviewing how it all looked in 1963 and outlining some of the possibilities for the future as they appear in 2000 with some prescriptions for action. I know that I no longer have the 20/20 vision I had in 1963, but it is still tempting to take a look at what may be coming down the road—a road I see filled with potholes, surrounded by bandits, and leading to no clear ultimate destination.

The fifth edition of *The Uses of the University* thus ends with a new chapter that compares the situations in 1963 and 2000. It is preceded by my original Godkin Lectures in Chapters 1, 2, and 3. Then follow additional essays, which I wrote covering developments at about ten-year intervals for the rest of the twentieth century, and which appeared in successive editions.

Chapter 4, written in 1972, consists of some of my reactions after the student revolts of the 1960s. My lectures in 1963 had become a target for student activists. They did not like the new university world that I described. The students neglected the fact that I also disliked the pathologies of this new world and was their first and prime critic. The "multiversity" became "Clark Kerr's monstrosity." It was even insinuated that I was a "proto-fascist ideologue."[1] This was then shortened into "fascist" on Berkeley's Sproul Plaza. One might conclude that it is wiser for a university president not to write at all, or to do so only in platitudes. I paid a heavy price for being an honest and realistic commentator.

Written in 1982, Chapter 5 looks back on the decade of attempted academic reforms that followed the student revolts, a period that produced many manifestos but few enduring results. In particular, "participatory democracy" as a method of university governance by activist faculty and students was only a flash in the pan. The major permanent reform was the creation of courses celebrating ethnic, racial, and gender diversities, usually affecting curricula in big universities at or below a one percent level. This experience with academic reform illustrated how radical some professors can be when they look at the external world and how conservative when they look inwardly at themselves—a split personality.

Chapter 6 is the first of three commentaries I added in the 1995 edition. Looking back, I now note their generally pessimistic tone: the demise of "liberal education" for undergraduates, the fractionalization of the campus by fields of study, by ideologies, by gender and ethnic status. At the same time, however, it was clear that the American university had become the supreme research institution in the world. It had taken the place of the German university that had led the world at the end of the nineteenth century and until World War I.

Nineteen sixty-three had been a period of euphoria, of buoyancy; by 1994, when I wrote the essay, the mood was more one of depression, of self doubt. Why this great change in spirit? The flow of resources had been reduced as the rate of economic productivity increases dropped below their historical levels. The federal government had exhausted its vast post–World War II enthusiasm for higher education as shown in support for research and development and student grants and loans.

Rapid increases in student enrollment had slowed, although the predicted "demographic depression" of the 1980s had never materialized.

The academic reform movement had fizzled out. The last great attempt to restore attention to undergraduates and their liberal education—at the University of California at Santa Cruz—was failing, as had the earlier Hutchins experiment at Chicago and the "Red Book" reforms at Harvard. The university community was splintering into a series of contending elements. An economic depression was reducing state support for higher education. "Lead, kindly light" in 1963 had turned into "encircling gloom" by 1994.

I did not realize at the time how great was the change in the mood of academe by the mid-1990s. It had become the worst of all possible worlds. Higher education had entered a depressive state by 1980 and remained there—the Great Academic Depression.

Chapter 7, also written in 1994, continues the discussion of this depression, particularly noting reduced external resources for higher education. It also laments the disintegration of the "guild" status of higher education and the decline of what Henry Rosovsky called professional "civic virtue."[2]

Chapter 8, the last of the commentaries added in the 1995 edition, went on to describe some of the hard choices that seemed to lie ahead, in particular, some that higher education had long faced but for which it had never found satisfactory conclusions. One was how to make better use of resources; another was how higher education might better assist primary and secondary education. However, I ended with a stance of guarded optimism in approaching the future of higher education in the United States, which is where I had started in 1963.

Chapter 9 brings this series of essays to an end. It has gone on so long due to the goodwill and continuing interest of the Harvard University Press and particularly of the editor Aida Donald to whom I dedicate these essays. This chapter sets forth some of the challenges that lie ahead, which dwarf, in their complexity, anything we faced in 1963. I end with what might be called "guarded confusion" but am convinced that new knowledge still makes the world go round and that the university is still its main source.

Universities in America are at a hinge of history: while connected with their past, they are swinging in another direction. This volume, based on the 1963 Godkin Lectures, delivered at Harvard University on April 23, 24, and 25, 1963, attempts to describe and to evaluate some of the significant new developments in American higher education. The title, "The Uses of the University," implies a generally optimistic tone, for it is not the *misuses* of the university that will mainly concern us. At the same time, however, it is well to note that in the discussion that follows, analysis should not be confused with approval or description with defense.

Although it is one of our oldest social institutions, the university today finds itself in a quite novel position in society. It faces its new role with few precedents to fall back on, with little but platitudes to mask the nakedness of the change. Instead of platitudes and nostalgic glances backward to what it once was, the university needs a rigorous look at the reality of the world it occupies today.

The basic reality, for the university, is the widespread recognition that new knowledge is the most important factor in economic and social growth. We are just now perceiving that the university's invisible product, knowledge, may be the most powerful single element in our culture, affecting the rise and fall of professions and even of social classes, of regions and even of nations.

Because of this fundamental reality, the university is being called upon to produce knowledge as never before—for civic and regional purposes, for national purposes, and even for no purpose at all beyond the realization that most knowledge eventually comes to serve mankind. And it is also being called upon to transmit knowledge to an unprecedented proportion of the population.

This reality is reshaping the very nature and quality of the university. Old concepts of faculty-student relations, of research, of faculty-administration roles are being changed at a rate without parallel. And this at a time when it seems that an entire generation is pounding at the gates and demanding admission. To the academician, conservative by nature, the sound made by the new generation often resembles the howl of a mob. To the politician, it is a signal to be obeyed. To the administrator, it is a warning that we are in new times and that the decisions we make now will be uncommonly productive—both of good and ill.

Thus the university has come to have a new centrality for all of us, as much for those who never see the ivied halls as for those who pass through them or reside there.

The university has been a remarkably unstudied institution until very recently. Seymour Harris was one of the first of my fellow economists to examine education as one might any other activity of society and to subject it to economic analysis. Today education, including higher education, is being scrutinized in all its aspects. This reflects the increasing recognition of its uses in economic growth, in international competition, in political and social as well as cultural development. One can only wonder whether the university was a better place before people began writing and talking so much about it—before they became so conscious of its uses.

THE USES OF THE UNIVERSITY

1

THE IDEA OF A MULTIVERSITY

The university started as a single community—a community of masters and students. It may even be said to have had a soul in the sense of a central animating principle. Today the large American university is, rather, a whole series of communities and activities held together by a common name, a common governing board, and related purposes. This great transformation is regretted by some, accepted by many, gloried in, as yet, by few. But it should be understood by all.

The university of today can perhaps be understood, in part, by comparing it with what it once was—with the academic cloister of Cardinal Newman, with the research organism of Abraham Flexner. Those are the ideal types from which it has derived, ideal types which still constitute the illusions of some of its inhabitants. The modern American university, however, is not Oxford nor is it Berlin; it is a new type of institution in the world. As a new type of institution, it is not really private and it is not really public; it is neither entirely of the world nor entirely apart from it. It is unique.

"The Idea of a University" was, perhaps, never so well expressed as by Cardinal Newman when engaged in founding the University of Dublin a little over a century ago.[1] His views reflected the Oxford of his day whence he had come. A university, wrote Cardinal Newman, is "the high protecting power of all knowledge and science, of fact and principle, of inquiry and discovery, of experiment and speculation; it maps out the territory of the intellect, and sees that . . . there is neither encroachment nor surrender on any side." He favored "liberal knowledge," and said that "useful knowledge" was a "deal of trash."

Newman was particularly fighting the ghost of Bacon who some 250 years before had condemned "a kind of adoration of the mind . . . by means whereof men have withdrawn themselves too much from the contemplation of nature, and the observations of experience, and have tumbled up and down in their own reason and conceits." Bacon believed that knowledge should be for the benefit and use of men, that it should "not be as a courtesan, for pleasure and vanity only, or as a bond-woman, to acquire and gain to her master's use; but as a spouse, for generation, fruit and comfort."[2]

To this Newman replied that "Knowledge is capable of being its own end. Such is the constitution of the human mind, that any kind of knowledge, if it really be such, is its own reward." And in a sharp jab at Bacon he said: "The Philosophy of Utility, you will say, Gentlemen, has at least done its work; and I grant it—it aimed low, but it has fulfilled its aim." Newman felt that other institutions should carry on research, for "If its object were scientific and philosophical discovery, I do not see why a University should have any students"—an observation sardonically echoed by today's students who often think their professors are not interested in them at all but only in research. A University training, said Newman, "aims at raising the intellectual tone of society, at cultivating the public mind, at purifying the national taste, at supplying true principles to popular enthusiasm and fixed aims to popular aspirations, at giving enlargement and sobriety to the ideas of the age, at facilitating the exercise of political powers, and refining the intercourse of private life." It prepares a man "to fill any post with credit, and to master any subject with facility."

This beautiful world was being shattered forever even as it was being so beautifully portrayed. By 1852, when Newman wrote, the German universities were becoming the new model. The democratic and industrial and scientific revolutions were all well underway in the western world. The gentleman "at home in any society" was soon to be at home in none. Science was beginning to take the place of moral philosophy, research the place of teaching.

"The Idea of a Modern University," to use Flexner's phrase,[3] was already being born. "A University," said Flexner in 1930, "is not outside, but inside the general social fabric of a given era. . . . It is not something apart, something historic, something that yields as little as possible to forces and influences that are more or less new. It is on the contrary . . . an expression of the age, as well as an influence operating upon both present and future."

It was clear by 1930 that "Universities have changed profoundly—and commonly in the direction of the social evolution of which they are part." This evolution had brought departments into universities, and still new departments; institutes and ever more institutes; created vast research libraries; turned the philosopher on his log into a researcher in his laboratory or the library stacks; taken medicine out of the hands of the profession and put it into the hands of the scientists; and much more. Instead of the individual student, there were the needs of society;

instead of Newman's eternal "truths in the natural order," there was discovery of the new; instead of the generalist, there was the specialist. The university became, in the words of Flexner, "an institution consciously devoted to the pursuit of knowledge, the solution of problems, the critical appreciation of achievement and the training of men at a really high level." No longer could a single individual "master any subject"—Newman's universal liberal man was gone forever.

But as Flexner was writing of the "Modern University," it, in turn, was ceasing to exist. The Berlin of Humboldt was being violated just as Berlin had violated the soul of Oxford. The universities were becoming too many things. Flexner himself complained that they were "secondary schools, vocational schools, teacher-training schools, research centers, 'uplift' agencies, businesses—these and other things simultaneously." They engaged in "incredible absurdities," "a host of inconsequential things." They "needlessly cheapened, vulgarized and mechanized themselves." Worst of all, they became "'service stations' for the general public."

Even Harvard. "It is clear," calculated Flexner, "that of Harvard's total expenditures not more than one-eighth is devoted to the *central* university disciplines at the level at which a university ought to be conducted." He wondered: "Who has forced Harvard into this false path? No one. It does as it pleases; and this sort of thing pleases." It obviously did not please Flexner. He wanted Harvard to disown the Graduate School of Business and let it become, if it had to survive at all, the "Boston School of Business." He would also have banished all Schools of Journalism and Home Economics, football, correspondence courses, and much else.

It was not only Harvard and other American universities, but also London. Flexner asked "in what sense the University of London is a university at all." It was only "a federation."

By 1930, American universities had moved a long way from Flexner's "Modern University" where "The heart of a university is a graduate school of arts and sciences, the solidly professional schools (mainly, in America, medicine and law) and certain research institutes." They were becoming less and less like a "genuine university," by which Flexner meant "an organism, characterized by highness and definiteness of aim, unity of spirit and purpose." The "Modern University" was as nearly dead in 1930 when Flexner wrote about it as the old Oxford was in 1852 when Newman idealized it. History moves faster than the observer's pen. Neither the ancient classics and theology nor the German philosophers and scientists could set the tone for the really modern university—the multiversity.

"The Idea of a Multiversity" has no bard to sing its praises; no prophet to proclaim its vision; no guardian to protect its sanctity. It has its critics, its detractors, its transgressors. It also has its barkers selling its wares to all who will listen—and many do. But it also has its reality rooted in the logic of history. It is an imperative rather than a reasoned choice among elegant alternatives.

President Nathan Pusey wrote in his latest annual report to the members of the Harvard Board of Overseers that the average date of graduation of the present Board members was 1924; and much has happened to Harvard since 1924. Half of the buildings are new. The faculty has grown five-fold, the budget nearly fifteen-fold. "One can find almost anywhere one looks similar examples of the effect wrought in the curriculum and in the nature of the contemporary university by widening international awareness, advancing knowledge, and increasingly sophisticated methods of research. . . . Asia and Africa, radio telescopes, masers and lasers and devices for interplanetary exploration unimagined in 1924—these and other developments have effected such enormous changes in the intellectual orientation and aspiration of the contemporary university as to have made the university we knew as students now seem a strangely underdeveloped, indeed a very simple and an almost unconcerned kind of institution. And the pace of change continues."[4]

Not only at Harvard. The University of California last year had operating expenditures from all sources of nearly half a billion dollars, with almost another 100 million for construction; a total employment of over 40,000 people, more than IBM and in a far greater variety of endeavors; operations in over a hundred locations, counting campuses, experiment stations, agricultural and urban extension centers, and projects abroad involving more than fifty countries; nearly 10,000 courses in its catalogues; some form of contact with nearly every industry, nearly every level of government, nearly every person in its region. Vast amounts of expensive equipment were serviced and maintained. Over 4,000 babies were born in its hospitals. It is the world's largest purveyor of white mice. It will soon have the world's largest primate colony. It will soon also have 100,000 students—30,000 of them at the graduate level; yet much less than one third of its expenditures are directly related to teaching. It already has nearly 200,000 students in extension courses—including one out of every three lawyers and one out of every six doctors in the state. And Harvard and California are illustrative of many more.

Newman's "Idea of a University" still has its devotees—chiefly the humanists and the generalists and the undergraduates. Flexner's "Idea of a Modern University" still has its supporters—chiefly the scientists and the specialists and the graduate students. "The

Idea of a Multiversity" has its practitioners—chiefly the administrators, who now number many of the faculty among them, and the leadership groups in society at large. The controversies are still around in the faculty clubs and the student coffee houses; and the models of Oxford and Berlin and modern Harvard all animate segments of what was once a "community of masters and students" with a single vision of its nature and purpose. These several competing visions of true purpose, each relating to a different layer of history, a different web of forces, cause much of the malaise in the university communities of today. The university is so many things to so many different people that it must, of necessity, be partially at war with itself.

How did the multiversity happen? No man created it; in fact, no man visualized it. It has been a long time coming about and it has a long way to go. What is its history? How is it governed? What is life like within it? What is its justification? Does it have a future?

The Strands of History

The multiversity draws on many strands of history. To the extent that its origins can be identified, they can be traced to the Greeks. But there were several traditions even then. Plato had his Academy devoted to truth largely for its own sake, but also truth for the philosophers who were to be kings. The Sophists, whom Plato detested so much that he gave them an evil aura persisting to this day, had their schools too. These schools taught rhetoric and other useful skills—they were more interested in attainable success in life than they were in the unattainable truth. The Pythagoreans were concerned, among other things, with mathematics and astronomy. The modern academician likes to trace his intellectual forebears to the groves of Academe; but the modern university with its professional schools and scientific institutes might look equally to the Sophists and the Pythagoreans. The humanists, the professionals, and the scientists all have their roots in ancient times. The "Two Cultures" or the "Three Cultures" are almost as old as culture itself.

Despite its Greek precursors, however, the university is, as Hastings Rashdall wrote, "a distinctly medieval institution."[5] In the Middle Ages it developed many of the features that prevail today—a name and a central location, masters with a degree of autonomy, students, a system of lectures, a procedure for examinations and degrees, and even an administrative structure with its "faculties." Salerno in medicine, Bologna in law, and Paris in theology and philosophy were the great pacesetters. The university came to be a center for the professions, for the study of the classics, for theological and philosophical disputes. Oxford and Cambridge, growing out of Paris, developed in their distinctive ways with their particular emphasis on the residential college instead of the separate faculties as the primary unit.

By the end of the eighteenth century the European universities had long since become oligarchies, rigid in their subject matter, centers of reaction in their societies—opposed, in large part, to the Reformation, unsympathetic to the spirit of creativity of the Renaissance, antagonistic to the new science. There was something almost splendid in their disdain for contemporary events. They stood like castles without windows, profoundly introverted. But the tides of change can cut very deep. In France the universities were swept away by the Revolution, as they almost had been in England at the time of Cromwell.

It was in Germany that the rebirth of the university took place. Halle had dropped teaching exclusively in Latin in 1693; Göttingen had started the teaching of history in 1736; but it was the establishment of Berlin by Wilhelm von Humboldt in 1809 from his vantage point in the Prussian Ministry that was the dramatic event. The emphasis was on philosophy and science, on research, on graduate instruction, on the freedom of professors and students (*Lehrfreiheit* and *Lernfreiheit*). The department was created, and the institute. The professor was established as a great figure within and without the university. The Berlin plan spread rapidly throughout Germany, which was then entering a period of industrialization and intense nationalism following the shock of the defeat at the hands of Napoleon. The university carried with it two great new forces: science and nationalism. It is true that the German university system later bogged down through its uncritical reliance on the great professional figure who ruled for life over his department and institute, and that it could be subverted by Hitler because of its total dependence on the state. But this does not vitiate the fact that the German university in the nineteenth century was one of the vigorous new institutions in the world.

In 1809 when Berlin was founded, the United States already had a number of colleges developed on the model of the colleges at Oxford and Cambridge. They concentrated on Calvinism for the would-be preacher and classics for the young gentleman. Benjamin Franklin had had other ideas for the University of Pennsylvania, then the College of Philadelphia, in the 1750's.[6] Reflecting Locke, he wanted "a *more useful* culture of young minds." He was interested in training people for agriculture and commerce; in exploring science. Education should "serve mankind." These ideas were not to take root for another century. Drawing on the French Enlightenment, Jefferson started the University of Virginia with a broad curriculum including mathematics and science, and with the electives that Eliot was to make so famous at Harvard half a century later. He put great emphasis on a library—an almost revolutionary idea at the time. Again the application of the ideas was to be long delayed.

The real line of development for the modern American university began with Professor George Ticknor at Harvard in 1825. He tried to reform Harvard on the model of Göttingen where he had studied, and found that reforming Harvard must wait for an Eliot with forty years and the powers of the presidency at his disposal. Yale at the time was the great center of reaction—its famous faculty report of 1828 was a ringing proclamation to do nothing, or at least nothing that had not always been done at Yale or by God.[7] Francis Wayland at Brown in the 1850's made a great fight for the German system, including a program of electives, as did Henry Tappan at Michigan—both without success.

Then the breakthrough came. Daniel Coit Gilman, disenchanted with the then grim prospects at California, became the first president of the new university of Johns Hopkins in 1876. The institution began as a graduate school with an emphasis on research. For Flexner, Gilman was the great hero-figure—and Johns Hopkins "the most stimulating influence that higher education in America had ever known." Charles W. Eliot at Harvard followed the Gilman breakthrough and Harvard during his period (1869 to 1909) placed great emphasis on the graduate school, the professional school, and research—it became a university. But Eliot made his own particular contribution by establishing the elective system permitting students to choose their own courses of study. Others quickly followed—Andrew Dickson White at Cornell, James B. Angell at Michigan, Frederick Barnard at Columbia, William W. Folwell at Minnesota, David Starr Jordan at Stanford, William Rainey Harper at Chicago, Charles K. Adams at Wisconsin, Benjamin Ide Wheeler at California. The state universities, just then expanding, followed the Hopkins idea. Yale and Princeton trailed behind.

The Hopkins idea brought with it the graduate school with exceptionally high academic standards in what was still a rather new and raw civilization; the renovation of professional education, particularly in medicine; the establishment of the preeminent influence of the department; the creation of research institutes and centers, of university presses and learned journals and the "academic ladder"; and also the great proliferation of courses. If students were to be free to choose their courses (one aspect of the *Lernfreiheit* of the early nineteenth-century German university), then professors were free to offer their wares (as *Lehrfreiheit*, the other great slogan of the developing German universities of a century and a half ago, essentially assured). The elective system, however, came more to serve the professors than the students for whom it was first intended, for it meant that the curriculum was no longer controlled by educational policy as the Yale faculty in 1828 had insisted that it should be. Each professor had his own interests, each professor wanted the status of having his own special course, each professor got his own course—and university catalogues came to include 3,000 or more of them. There was, of course, as a result of the new research, more knowledge to spread over the 3,000 courses; otherwise the situation would have been impossible. In any event, freedom for the student to choose became freedom for the professor to invent; and the professor's love of specialization has become the student's hate of fragmentation. A kind of bizarre version of academic laissez-faire has emerged. The student, unlike Adam Smith's idealized buyer, *must* consume—usually at the rate of fifteen hours a week. The modern university was born.

Along with the Hopkins experiment came the land grant movement—and these two influences turned out to be more compatible than might at first appear. The one was Prussian, the other American; one elitist, the other democratic; one academically pure, the other sullied by contact with the soil and the machine. The one looked to Kant and Hegel, the other to Franklin, Jefferson, and Lincoln. But they both served an industrializing nation and they both did it through research and the training of technical competence. Two strands of history were woven together in the modern American university. Michigan became a German-style university and Harvard a land grant type of institution, without the land.

The land grant movement brought schools of agriculture and engineering (in Germany relegated to the *Technische Hochschulen*), of home economics and business administration; opened the doors of universities to the children of farmers and workers, as well as of the middle and upper classes; introduced agricultural experiment stations and service bureaus. Allan Nevins in commenting on the Morrill Act of 1862 said: "The law annexed wide neglected areas to the domain of instruction. Widening the gates of opportunity, it made democracy freer, more adaptable and more kinetic."[8]

A major new departure in the land grant movement came before World War I when the land grant universities extended their activities beyond their campus boundaries. "The Wisconsin Idea" came to flower under the progressivism of the first Roosevelt and the first La Follette. The University of Wisconsin, particularly during the presidency of Charles Van Hise (1903 to 1918), entered the legislative halls in Madison with reform programs, supported the trade union movement through John R. Commons, developed agricultural and urban extension as never before. The university served the whole state. Other state universities did likewise. Even private universities, like Chicago and Columbia, developed important extension programs.

New contacts with the community were created. University athletics became, particularly in the 1920's, a form of public entertainment, which is not unknown even in the 1960's, even in the Ivy League. Once started, university spectator sports could not be killed even by the worst of teams or the best of deemphasis; and few universities seriously sought after either.

A counterrevolution against these developments was occasionally waged. A. Lawrence Lowell at Harvard (1909 to 1934) emphasized the undergraduate houses and concentration of course work, as against the graduate work and electives of Eliot. It is a commentary not just on Harvard but also on the modern American university that Eliot and Lowell could look in opposite directions and the same institution could follow them both and glory in it. Universities have a unique capacity for riding off in all directions and still staying in the same place, as Harvard has so decisively demonstrated. At Chicago, long after Lowell, Robert M. Hutchins tried to take the university back to Cardinal Newman, to Thomas Aquinas, and to Plato and Aristotle. He succeeded in reviving the philosophic dialogue he loves so well and practices so expertly; but Chicago went on being a modern American university.

Out of the counterreformation, however, came a great new emphasis on student life—particularly undergraduate. Earnest attempts were made to create American counterparts of Oxford and Cambridge; residence halls, student unions, intramural playfields, undergraduate libraries, counseling centers sprang up in many places during the thirties, forties, and fifties. This was a long way from the pure German model, which had provided the student with only the professor and the classroom, and which had led Tappan to abolish dormitories at Michigan. British influence was back, as it was also with the introduction of honors programs, tutorials, independent study.

Out of all these fragments, experiments, and conflicts a kind of unlikely consensus has been reached. Undergraduate life seeks to follow the British, who have done the best with it, and an historical line that goes back to Plato; the humanists often find their sympathies here. Graduate life and research follow the Germans, who once did best with them, and an historical line that goes back to Pythagoras; the scientists lend their support to all this. The "lesser" professions (lesser than law and medicine) and the service activities follow the American pattern, since the Americans have been best at them, and an historical line that goes back to the Sophists; the social scientists are most likely to be sympathetic. Lowell found his greatest interest in the first, Eliot in the second, and James Bryant Conant (1934 to 1954) in the third line of development and in the synthesis. The resulting combination does not seem plausible but it has given America a remarkably effective educational institution. A university any-where can aim no higher than to be as British as possible for the sake of the undergraduates, as German as possible for the sake of the graduates and the research personnel, as American as possible for the sake of the public at large—and as confused as possible for the sake of the preservation of the whole uneasy balance.

The Governance of the Multiversity

The multiversity is an inconsistent institution. It is not one com-munity but several—the community of the undergraduate and the community of the graduate; the community of the humanist, the community of the social scientist, and the community of the scientist; the communities of the professional schools; the com-munity of all the nonacademic personnel; the community of the administrators. Its edges are fuzzy—it reaches out to alumni, legislators, farmers, businessmen, who are all related to one or more of these internal communities. As an institution, it looks far into the past and far into the future, and is often at odds with the present. It serves society almost slavishly—a society it also criticizes, sometimes unmercifully. Devoted to equality of oppor-tunity, it is itself a class society. A community, like the medieval communities of masters and students, should have common interests; in the multiversity, they are quite varied, even conflicting. A community should have a soul, a single animating principle; the multiversity has several—some of them quite good, although there is much debate on which souls really deserve salvation.

The multiversity is a name. This means a great deal more than it sounds as though it might. The name of the institution stands for a certain standard of performance, a certain degree of respect, a certain historical legacy, a characteristic quality of spirit. This is of the utmost importance to faculty and to students, to the government agencies and the industries with which the institution deals. Protection and enhancement of the prestige of the name are central to the multiversity. How good is its reputation, what John J. Corson calls its "institutional character"?[9]

Flexner thought of a university as an "organism." In an organism, the parts and the whole are inextricably bound together. Not so the multiversity—many parts can be added and subtracted with little effect on the whole or even little notice taken or any blood spilled. It is more a mechanism—a series of processes producing a series of results—a mechanism held together by administrative rules and powered by money.

Hutchins once described the modern university as a series of separate schools and departments held together by a central heating system. In an area where heating is less important and the automobile more, I have sometimes thought of it as a series of individual faculty entrepreneurs held together by a common grievance over parking.

It is, also, a system of government like a city, or a city state: the city state of the multiversity. It may be inconsistent but it must be governed—not as the guild it once was, but as a complex entity with greatly fractionalized power. There are several competitors for this power.

The students. The students had all the power once; that was in Bologna. Their guilds ran the university and dominated the masters. And the students were tougher on the masters than the masters have ever been on the students. The Bologna pattern had an impact on Salamanca and Spain generally and then in Latin America, where students to this day are usually found in the top governing councils. Their impact is generally more to lower than to raise academic standards although there are exceptions such as Buenos Aires after Peron under the leadership of Risieri Frondizi. Students also involve the university as an institution in the national political controversies of the moment.

Jefferson tried a system of student self-government in the 1820's but quickly abandoned it when all the professors tendered their resignations. He favored self-government by both students and faculty, but never discovered how both could have it at the same time—nor has anybody else. Although José Ortega y Gasset, in addressing the student federation at the University of Madrid, was willing to turn over the entire "mission of the university" to the students, he neglected to comment on faculty reaction.[10]

As part of the "Wisconsin idea" before World War I, there was quite a wave of creation of student governments. They found their power in the area of extracurricular activities, where it has remained. Their extracurricular programs helped broaden student life in such diverse fields as debating, theatrical productions, literary magazines.

Students do have considerable strictly academic influence, however, quite beyond that with which they are usually credited. The system of electives gives them a chance to help determine in which areas and disciplines a university will grow. Their choices, as consumers, guide university expansion and contraction, and this process is far superior to a more rigid guild system of producer determination as in medicine where quotas are traditional. Also students, by their patronage, designate the university teachers. The faculty may, in fact, appoint the faculty, but within this faculty group the students choose the real teachers. In a large university a quarter of the faculty may be selected by the students to do half or more of the actual teaching; the students also "select" ten percent or more to do almost none at all.

The faculty. The guilds of masters organized and ran the University of Paris, and later they did the same at Oxford and Cambridge. Faculty control at Oxford and Cambridge, through the colleges, has remained stronger than anywhere else over the centuries, but even there it has been greatly diminished in recent times.

In the United States, the first great grant of power to the faculty of a major university was at Yale when Jeremiah Day was president (1817 to 1846). It was during the Day regime that the Yale faculty report of 1828 was issued. Harvard has had, by contrast, as McGeorge Bundy has said in his inimitable style, "a tradition of quite high-handed and centralized executive behavior—and it has not suffered, in balance, as a consequence."[11]

Faculties generally in the United States and the British Commonwealth, some earlier and some later, have achieved authority over admissions, approval of courses, examinations, and granting of degrees—all handled in a rather routine fashion from the point of view of the faculty as a whole. They have also achieved considerable influence over faculty appointments and academic freedom, which are not handled routinely. Faculty control and influence in these areas are essential to the proper conduct of academic life. Once the elective system was established, educational policy became less important to the faculty, although, as at Harvard under Lowell, the elective system was modified to call for general rules on concentration and distribution of work. Since Harvard adopted its program for general education in

1945[12] and Hutchins left Chicago, there has been remarkably little faculty discussion of general educational policy. By contrast, there has been a great deal in England, particularly in the "new universities," where faculty discussion of educational policy has been very lively, and faculty influence, as a consequence, substantial.

Organized faculty control or influence over the general direction of growth of the American multiversity has been quite small, as illustrated by the development of the federal grant university. Individual faculty influence, however, has been quite substantial, even determinative, in the expanding areas of institutes and research grants. Still it is a long way from Paris at the time of Abelard.

Public authority. "Public" authority is a very mixed entity of emperors and popes, ministers of education, grants committees, trustees, and Royal Commissions. But almost everywhere, regardless of the origin of the system, there has come to be a public authority. Even in the Middle Ages, emperors and popes, dukes, cardinals, and city councils came to authorize or establish the universities to make them legitimate—the guild alone was not enough. When Henry VIII had trouble about a wife it shook Oxford and Cambridge to the core.

In modern times, Napoleon was the first to seize control of a university system. He completely reorganized it and made it part of the nationally administered educational system of France, as it remains to this day. He separated off research activities and special training institutions for teachers, engineers, and so forth. The universities became a series of loosely related professional schools. Not until the 1890's were the universities brought back together as meaningful entities and a measure of faculty control restored. Soviet Russia has followed the French pattern with even greater state control.

In Germany, the state governments traditionally have controlled the universities in great detail. So also has the government in Italy. In Latin America a degree of formal autonomy from the government has either been retained or attained, although informal reality usually contradicts the theory.

Even in Great Britain, the "public" has moved in on the faculties. Royal Commissions have helped modernize Oxford and Cambridge. The Redbrick and Scottish universities and London either have had from the beginning or acquired governing boards of a mixed nature, including lay members representative of public authority. Since 1919, and particularly since World War II, the University Grants Committee has made its influence felt in a less and less gentle and more and more effective way.

The lay board has been the distinctive American device for "public" authority in connection with universities, although the device was used in Holland in the late sixteenth century. Beyond the lay board in the state universities are the state department of finance and the governor and the legislature with a tendency toward increasingly detailed review.

Richard Hofstadter has made the interesting observation that the first lay board and the first effective concept of academic freedom developed in Holland at the same time; and that academic freedom has never been inherited from some Golden Age of the past but has instead been imported from the institutions of the surrounding society.[13]

Through all these devices, public influences have been asserted in university affairs. Public influence has increased as much in Paris as student influence has declined in Bologna. Everywhere, with the decreasing exception of Oxford and Cambridge, the ultimate authority lies in the "public" domain; everywhere, with a few exceptions, it is fortunately not exercised in an ultimate fashion. We have, however, come a long way from the guilds of masters, the guilds of students, the guilds of masters and students. The location of power has generally moved from inside to outside the original community of masters and students. The nature of the multiversity makes it inevitable that this historical transfer will not be reversed in any significant fashion, although the multiversity does permit the growth of subcultures which can be relatively autonomous and can have an impact on the totality.

The distribution of power is of great importance. In Germany it came to be lodged too completely in the figure of the full professor at one end and the minister of education at the other; in Oxford and Cambridge, at one time, in an oligarchy of professors; in the United States, during a substantial period, almost exclusively in the president; in Latin America, too often, in the students within and the politicians without.

Influences—external and semi-external. Beyond the formal structure of power, as lodged in students, faculty, administration, or "public" instrumentalities, lie the sources of informal influence. The American system is particularly sensitive to the pressures of its many particular publics. Continental and British universities are less intertwined with their surrounding societies than the American and thus more inward-looking and self-contained. When "the borders of the campus are the boundaries of our state," the lines dividing what is internal from what is external become quite blurred; taking the campus to the state brings the state to the campus. In the so-called "private" universities, alumni, donors, foundations, the federal agencies, the professional and business communities bulk large among the semi-external influences; and in the so-called "public" universities, the agricultural, trade union, and public school communities are likely to be added to the list, and also a more searching press. The multiversity has many "publics" with many interests; and by the very nature of the multiversity many of these interests are quite legitimate and others are quite frivolous.

The administration.   The original medieval universities had at the start nothing that could be identified as a separate administration, but one quickly developed. The guild of masters or students selected a rector; and later there were deans of the faculties. At Oxford and Cambridge, there came to be the masters of the colleges. In more modern times in France, Germany, and Italy, the rector has come to stand between the faculty and the minister of education, closer to the minister of education in France and closer to the faculty in Germany; internally he has served principally as chairman of the council of deans where deans still retain substantial authority as in France and Italy. In Germany the full professor, chairman of his department, director of his institute, is a figure of commanding authority.

Even in England, even in Oxford and Cambridge, the central administration is attaining more influence—the vice chancellorship can no longer be rotated casually among the masters. The vice chancellor now must deal with the university grants committee and the vice chancellors of the other universities. The university itself is a much more important unit with its research laboratories, central library, its lecturers in specialized subjects; the college is much less self-contained than it was. All of this has created something of a crisis in the administration of Oxford and Cambridge where administrators once were not to be seen or heard and the work was accomplished by a handful of clerks working in a Dickensian office. Oxbridge is becoming more like the Redbricks. London is *sui generis*.

The general rule is that the administration everywhere becomes, by force of circumstances if not by choice, a more prominent feature of the university. As the institution becomes larger, administration becomes more formalized and separated as a distinct function; as the institution becomes more complex, the role of administration becomes more central in integrating it; as it becomes more related to the once external world, the administration assumes the burdens of these relationships. The managerial revolution has been going on also in the university.

Multiversity President, Giant or Mediator-Initiator?

It is sometimes said that the American multiversity president is a two-faced character. This is not so. If he were, he could not survive. He is a many-faced character, in the sense that he must face in many directions at once while contriving to turn his back on no important group. In this he is different in degree from his counterparts of rectors and vice chancellors, since they face in fewer directions because their institutions have fewer doors and windows to the outside world. The difference, however, is not one of kind. And intensities of relationships vary greatly; the rector of a Latin American university, from this point of view, may well have the most trying task of all, though he is less intertwined in a range of relationships than the North American university president.

The university president in the United States is expected to be a friend of the students, a colleague of the faculty, a good fellow with the alumni, a sound administrator with the trustees, a good speaker with the public, an astute bargainer with the foundations and the federal agencies, a politician with the state legislature, a friend of industry, labor, and agriculture, a persuasive diplomat with donors, a champion of education generally, a supporter of the professions (particularly law and medicine), a spokesman to the press, a scholar in his own right, a public servant at the state and national levels, a devotee of opera and football equally, a decent human being, a good husband and father, an active member of a church. Above all he must enjoy traveling in airplanes, eating his meals in public, and attending public ceremonies. No one can be all of these things. Some succeed at being none.

He should be firm, yet gentle; sensitive to others, insensitive to himself; look to the past and the future, yet be firmly planted in the present; both visionary and sound; affable, yet reflective; know the value of a dollar and realize that ideas cannot be bought; inspiring in his visions yet cautious in what he does; a man of principle yet able to make a deal; a man with broad perspective who will follow the details conscientiously; a good American but ready to criticize the status quo fearlessly; a seeker of truth where the truth may not hurt too much; a source of public policy pronouncements when they do not reflect on his own institution. He should sound like a mouse at home and look like a lion abroad. He is one of the marginal men in a democratic society—of whom there are many others—on the margin of many groups, many ideas, many endeavors, many characteristics. He is a marginal man but at the very center of the total process.

Who is he really?

To Flexner, he was a hero-figure, "a daring pioneer" who filled an "impossible post" yet some of his accomplishments were "little short of miraculous"; thus the "forceful president"—the Gilman, the Eliot, the Harper. The necessary revolutions came from on high. There should be Giants in the Groves. To Thorstein Veblen he was a "Captain of Erudition,"[14] and Veblen did not think well of captains. To Upton Sinclair, the university president was "the most universal faker and most variegated prevaricator that has yet appeared in the civilized world."[15]

To the faculty, he is usually not a hero-figure. Hutchins observed that the faculty really "prefer anarchy to any form of government"[16]—particularly the presidential form.

The issue is whether the president should be "leader" or "officeholder," as Hutchins phrased it; "educator" or "caretaker," as Harold W. Dodds[17] stated it; "creator" or "inheritor," as Frederick Rudolph[18] saw it; "initiator" as viewed by James L.

Morrill[19] or consensus-seeker as viewed by John D. Millett;[20] the wielder of power or the persuader, as visualized by Henry M. Wriston;[21] "pump" or "bottleneck" as categorized by Eric Ashby.[22]

The case for leadership has been strongly put by Hutchins. A university needs a purpose, "a vision of the end." If it is to have a "vision," the president must identify it; and, without vision, there is "aimlessness" and the "vast chaos of the American university." "The administrator must accept a special responsibility for the discussion, clarification, definition and proclamation of this end." He must be a "troublemaker, for every change in education is a change in the habits of some members of the faculty." For all this he needs the great "moral virtues" of "courage," "fortitude," "justice," and "prudence." In looking for administrators who really thought and wrote about the "end" of their institution, Hutchins particularly identified Marcus Aurelius as the great prototype.[23] Lowell, too, believed a president should have a "plan" and that although the faculty was "entitled to propose changes," the plan should not basically be subject to interference. He also had the rather quaint idea that the president should "never feel hurried" or "work . . . under pressure."[24]

There were such leaders in higher education. Hutchins was one. Lowell was another; and so was Eliot. When Eliot was asked by a faculty member of the medical school how it could be after eighty years of managing its own affairs the faculty had to accommodate to so many changes, he could answer, "There is a new president."[25] Even in Oxford, of all places, as it belatedly adapted to the new world of scholarship, Benjamin Jowett as Master of Balliol could set as his rule: "Never retract, never explain. Get it done and let them howl."[26] Lord Bryce could comment in his *American Commonwealth* on the great authority of the president in the American university, on his "almost monarchical position."[27]

But the day of the monarchs has passed—the day when Benjamin Ide Wheeler could ride his white horse across the Berkeley campus or Nicholas Murray Butler rule from Morningside Heights. Flexner rather sadly recorded that "the day of the excessively autocratic president is . . . over. He has done a great service . . ." Paul Lazarsfeld could observe the "academic power vacuum" that resulted—leadership no longer taken by the president nor assumed by the faculty, with the result of little "institutional development."[28] Hutchins was the last of the giants in the sense that he was the last of the university presidents who really tried to change his institution and higher education in any fundamental way. Instead of the not always so agreeable autocracy, there is now the usually benevolent bureaucracy, as in so much of the rest of the world. Instead of the Captain of Erudition or even David Riesman's "staff sergeant," there is the Captain of the Bureaucracy who is sometimes a galley slave on his own ship; and "no great revolutionary figure is likely to appear."[29]

The role of giant was never a happy one. Hutchins concluded that the administrator has many ways to lose, and no way to win, and came to acknowledge that patience, which he once called a "delusion and a snare," was also a virtue. "It is one thing to get things done. It is another to make them last." The experience of Tappan at Michigan was typical of many, as Angell later saw it: "Tappan was the largest figure of a man that ever appeared on the Michigan campus. And he was stung to death by gnats."[30]

The giant was seldom popular with the faculty and was often bitterly opposed, as in the "revolution" against Wheeler at California. And faculty government gained strength as faculties gained distinction. The experiences of Tappan, Wheeler, Hutchins, even Thomas Jefferson, are part of the lore of the university presidency. So are those of Wayland, who resigned from Brown in frustration after vainly trying something new, Woodrow Wilson with all his battles over innovations at Princeton, and many others.

Moreover, the university has changed; it has become bigger and more complex, more tensed with checks and balances. As Rudolph saw it, there came to be "a delicate balance of interests, a polite tug of war, a blending of emphases." The presidency was "an office fraught with so many perils, shot through with so many ambiguities, an office that was many things to many men."[31] There are more elements to conciliate, fewer in a position to be led. The university has become the multiversity and the nature of the presidency has followed this change.

Also, the times have changed. The giants were innovators during a wave of innovation, to use the terms of Joseph Schumpeter drawn from another context. The American university required vast renovation to meet the needs of the changing and growing nation. As Eliot said in his inaugural address, "The University must accommodate itself promptly to significant changes in the character of the people for whom it exists." The title of Wilson's inaugural address was, "Princeton for the Nation's Service." They and others helped take what had been denominational colleges and turn them into modern national universities. They were not inventors—the Germans did the inventing—but they came along at a stage in history when massive innovation was the order of the day. The giants today, when found at all, are more likely to be in a few of the old Latin American universities undergoing modernization or the new British universities in the midst of an intense discussion of educational policy.

The giants had performed "a great service," but gentler hands were needed. University administration reverted to the more standard British model of "government by consent and after consultation."[32] There is a "kind of lawlessness"[33] in any large university with many separate sources of initiative and power; and the task is to keep this lawlessness within reasonable bounds. The president must seek "consensus" in a situation where there is a "struggle for power" among groups that share it.[34] "The president must use power economically, and persuasion to the fullest extent."[35] As Allan Nevins sees it, "The sharpest strain on growth lies not in finding the teachers, but expert administrators," and the new type of president required by the large universities "will be a coordinator rather than a creative leader . . . an expert executive, a tactful moderator. . . ."[36]

Academic government has taken the form of the Guild, as in the colleges of Oxford and Cambridge until recent times; of the Manor, as in Columbia under Butler; and of the United Nations, as in the modern multiversity. There are several "nations" of students, of faculty, of alumni, of trustees, of public groups. Each has its territory, its jurisdiction, its form of government. Each can declare war on the others; some have the power of veto. Each can settle its own problems by a majority vote, but altogether they form no single constituency. It is a pluralistic society with multiple cultures. Coexistence is more likely than unity. Peace is one priority item, progress another.

The president in the multiversity is leader, educator, creator, initiator, wielder of power, pump; he is *also* officeholder, caretaker, inheritor, consensus-seeker, persuader, bottleneck. But he is mostly a mediator.

The first task of the mediator is peace—how he may "the Two-and-Seventy jarring Sects confute." Peace within the student body, the faculty, the trustees; and peace between and among them. Peace between the "Two Cultures" and the "Three Cultures" and their subcultures; among all the ideas competing for support. Peace between the internal environment of the academic community and the external society that surrounds and sometimes almost engulfs it. But peace has its attributes. There is the "workable compromise" of the day that resolves the current problem. Beyond this lies the effective solution that enhances the long-run distinction and character of the institution. In seeking it, there are some things that should not be compromised, like freedom and quality—then the mediator needs to become the gladiator. The dividing lines between these two roles may not be as clear as crystal, but they are at least as fragile.

The second task is progress; institutional and personal survival are not enough. A multiversity is inherently a conservative institution but with radical functions. There are so many groups with a legitimate interest in the status quo, so many veto groups; yet the university must serve a knowledge explosion and a population explosion simultaneously. The president becomes the central mediator among the values of the past, the prospects for the future, and the realities of the present. He is the mediator among groups and institutions moving at different rates of speed and sometimes in different directions; a carrier of change—as infectious and sometimes as feared as a "Typhoid Mary." He is not an innovator for the sake of innovation, but he must be sensitive to the fruitful innovation. He has no new and bold "vision of the end." He is driven more by necessity than by voices in the air. "Innovation" may be the historical "measurement of success," the great characterizing feature of the "giants of the past";[37] but innovations sometimes succeed best when they have no obvious author. Lowell once observed that a president "cannot both do things and get credit for them"—that he should not "cackle like a hen that laid an egg."

The ends are already given—the preservation of the eternal truths, the creation of new knowledge, the improvement of service wherever truth and knowledge of high order may serve the needs of man. The ends are there; the means must be ever improved in a competitive dynamic environment. There is no single "end" to be discovered; there are several ends and many groups to be served.

The quality of the mediation is subject to judgment on two grounds, the keeping of the peace and the furthering of progress—the resolution of inter-personal and inter-group warfare, and the reconciliation of the tug of the anchor to the past with the pull of the Holy Grail of the future. Unfortunately peace and progress are more frequently enemies than friends; and since, in the long run, progress is more important than peace to a university, the effective mediator must, at times, sacrifice peace to progress. The ultimate test is whether the mediation permits progress to be made fast enough and in the right directions, whether the needed innovations take precedence over the conservatism of the institution. Mediators, though less dramatic than giants, are not a homogenized group; they only look that way.

They also appear to some people to be doing very little of consequence. Yet their role is absolutely essential if carried out constructively. They serve something of the function of the clerk of the meeting for the Quakers—the person who keeps the business moving, draws forth ideas, seeks the "sense of the meeting." David Riesman has suggested the term "evocator." The techniques must be those of the mediator; but to the techniques may also be added the goals of the innovator. The essence of the role, when adequately performed, is perhaps best conveyed by the term "mediator-initiator."

Power is not necessary to the task, though there must be a consciousness of power. The president must police its use by the constituent groups, so that none will have too much or too little or use it too unwisely. To make the multiversity work really effectively, the moderates need to be in control of each power center and there needs to be an attitude of tolerance between and among the power centers, with few territorial ambitions. When the extremists get in control of the students, the faculty, or the trustees with class warfare concepts, then the "delicate balance of interests" becomes an actual war.

The usual axiom is that power should be commensurate with responsibility, but, for the president, the *opportunity to persuade* should be commensurate with the responsibility. He must have ready access to each center of power, a fair chance in each forum of opinion, a chance to paint reality in place of illusion and to argue the cause of reason as he sees it.

Not all presidents seek to be constructive mediators amid their complexities. One famous president of a New York university succeeded in being at home only five months in five years. Some find it more pleasant to attend meetings, visit projects abroad, even give lectures at other universities; and at home they attend ceremonial functions, go to the local clubs, and allow the winds of controversy to swirl past them. Others look for "visions." But most presidents are in the control tower helping the real pilots make their landings without crashes, even in the fog.

Hutchins wrote of the four moral virtues for a university president. I should like to suggest a slightly different three—judgment, courage, and fortitude—but the greatest of these is fortitude since others have so little charity. The mediator, whether in government or industry or labor relations or domestic quarrels, is always subject to some abuse. He wins few clear-cut victories; he must aim more at avoiding the worst than seizing the best. He must find satisfaction in being *equally* distasteful to each of his constituencies; he must reconcile himself to the harsh reality that successes are shrouded in silence while failures are spotlighted in notoriety. The president of the multiversity must be content to hold its constituent elements loosely together and to move the whole enterprise another foot ahead in what often seems an unequal race with history.

Life in the Multiversity

The "Idea of a University" was a village with its priests. The "Idea of a Modern University" was a town—a one-industry town—with its intellectual oligarchy. "The Idea of a Multiversity" is a city of infinite variety. Some get lost in the city; some rise to the top within it; most fashion their lives within one of its many subcultures. There is less sense of community than in the village but also less sense of confinement. There is less sense of purpose than within the town but there are more ways to excel. There are also more refuges of anonymity—both for the creative person and the drifter. As against the village and the town, the "city" is more like the totality of civilization as it has evolved and more an integral part of it; and movement to and from the surrounding society has been greatly accelerated. As in a city, there are many separate endeavors under a single rule of law.

The students in the "city" are older, more likely to be married, more vocationally oriented, more drawn from all classes and races than the students in the village;[38] and they find themselves in a most intensely competitive atmosphere. They identify less with the total community and more with its subgroups. Burton R. Clark and Martin Trow have a particularly interesting typology of these subcultures: the "collegiate" of the fraternities and sororities and the athletes and activities majors; the "academic" of the serious students; the "vocational" of the students seeking training for specific jobs; and the "nonconformist" of the political activists, the aggressive intellectuals, and the bohemians.[39] These subcultures are not mutually exclusive, and some of the fascinating pageantry of the multiversity is found in their interaction one on another.

The multiversity is a confusing place for the student. He has problems of establishing his identity and sense of security within it. But it offers him a vast range of choices, enough literally to stagger the mind. In this range of choices he encounters the opportunities and the dilemmas of freedom. The casualty rate is high. The walking wounded are many. *Lernfreiheit*—the freedom of the student to pick and choose, to stay or to move on—is triumphant.

Life has changed also for the faculty member. The multiversity is in the main stream of events. To the teacher and the researcher have been added the consultant and the administrator. Teaching is less central than it once was for most faculty members; research has become more important. This has given rise to what has been called the "nonteacher"[40]—"the higher a man's standing, the less he has to do with students"—and to a threefold class structure of what used to be "the faculty": those who only do research, those who only teach (and they are largely in an auxiliary role), and those who still do some of both. In one university I know, the proportions at the Ph.D. level or its equivalent are roughly one researcher to two teachers to four who do both.

Consulting work and other sources of additional income have given rise to what is called the "affluent professor," a category that does include some but by no means all of the faculty. Additionally, many faculty members, with their research assistants and teaching assistants, their departments and institutes, have become administrators. A professor's life has become, it is said, "a rat race of business and activity, managing contracts and projects, guiding teams and assistants, bossing crews of technicians, making numerous trips, sitting on committees for government agencies, and engaging in other distractions necessary to keep the whole frenetic business from collapse."[41]

The intellectual world has been fractionalized as interests have become much more diverse; and there are fewer common topics of conversation at the faculty clubs. Faculty government has become more cumbersome, more the avocation of active minorities; and there are real questions whether it can work effectively on a large scale, whether it can agree on more than preservation of the status quo. Faculty members are less members of the particular university and more colleagues within their national academic discipline groups.

But there are many compensations. "The American professoriate" is no longer, as Flexner once called it, "a proletariat." Salaries and status have risen considerably. The faculty member is more a fully participating member of society, rather than a creature on the periphery; some are at the very center of national and world events. Research opportunities have been enormously increased. The faculty member within the big mechanism and with all his opportunities has a new sense of independence from the domination of the administration or his colleagues; much administration has been effectively decentralized to the level of the individual professor. In particular, he has a choice of roles and mixtures of roles to suit his taste as never before. He need not leave the Groves for the Acropolis unless he wishes; but he can, if he wishes. He may even become, as some have, essentially a professional man with his home office and basic retainer on the campus of the multiversity but with his clients scattered from coast to coast. He can also even remain the professor of old, as many do. There are several patterns of life from which to choose. So the professor too has greater freedom. *Lehrfreiheit,* in the old German sense of the freedom of the professor to do as he pleases, also is triumphant.

What is the justification of the modern American multiversity? History is one answer. Consistency with the surrounding society is another. Beyond that, it has few peers in the preservation and dissemination and examination of the eternal truths; no living peers in the search for new knowledge; and no peers in all history among institutions of higher learning in serving so many of the segments of an advancing civilization. Inconsistent internally as an institution, it is consistently productive. Torn by change, it has the stability of freedom. Though it has not a single soul to call its own, its members pay their devotions to truth.

The multiversity in America is perhaps best seen at work, adapting and growing, as it responded to the massive impact of federal programs beginning with World War II. A vast transformation has taken place without a revolution, for a time almost without notice being taken. The multiversity has demonstrated how adaptive it can be to new opportunities for creativity; how responsive to money; how eagerly it can play a new and useful role; how fast it can change while pretending that nothing has happened at all; how fast it can neglect some of its ancient virtues. What are the current realities of the federal grant university?

2

THE REALITIES OF THE
FEDERAL GRANT
UNIVERSITY

Two great impacts, beyond all other forces, have molded the modern American university system and made it distinctive. Both impacts have come from sources outside the universities. Both have come primarily from the federal government. Both have come in response to national needs.

The first was the land grant movement. Abraham Lincoln signed the Morrill Act in 1862. This act set the tone for the development of American universities, both public and private, for most of the ensuing hundred years. It was one of the most seminal pieces of legislation ever enacted.

The land grant movement came in response to the rapid industrial and agricultural development of the United States that attained such momentum in the middle of the last century. Universities were to assist this development through training that went beyond the creation of "gentlemen," and of teachers, preachers, lawyers, and doctors; through research related to the technical advance of farming and manufacturing; through service to many and ultimately to almost all of the economic and political segments of society. The land grant movement was also responsive to a growing democratic, even egalitarian and populist, trend in the nation. Pursuing this trend, higher education was to be open to all qualified young people from all walks of life. It was to serve less the perpetuation of an elite class and more the creation of a relatively classless society, with the doors of opportunity open to all through education.

This was a dramatic break with earlier American traditions in higher education. It created a new social force in world history. Nowhere before had universities been so closely linked with the daily life of so much of their societies. The university campus came to be one of the most heavily traveled crossroads in America—an intersection traversed by farmers, businessmen, politicians, students from almost every corner of almost every state. The cloister and the ivory tower were destroyed by being thrown open to all qualified comers.

Supporting the impact of the land grant movement was the effect on American universities of the model supplied by Germany. This German model gave academic respectability and content to the "land grant" idea; and Harvard, a private university with a long academic tradition, could travel much the same path of development as Cornell, a newly established land grant institution. German intellectualism and American populism were merged in the new university. Pure intellect and raw pragmatism made an unlikely but successful alliance.

The second great impact on the universities began with federal support of scientific research during World War II. The wartime laboratories that were the forerunners of such continuing government-financed research centers as the Lincoln Laboratory at the Massachusetts Institute of Technology, the Argonne at Chicago, and the Lawrence Radiation Laboratory at California, opened a new age. The major universities were enlisted in national defense and in scientific and technological development as never before. (In World War I the universities had only been a source of raw recruits.)

Instead of Gilman, Eliot, and White, there were now such new pioneers as Conant, Compton, and Bush to guide this alliance of the federal government with the universities. Don K. Price notes that "in the hands of Vannevar Bush, James B. Conant, and Karl T. Compton the government contract became a new type of federalism."[1] In addition to the industrial revolution there was now the scientific revolution to be served. In addition to the stimulus of Germany, there was Russia—for Russian scientific achievements both before and after Sputnik were an immense spur to the new departure. American universities have been changed almost as much by the federal research grant as by the land grant idea.

It is interesting that American universities, which pride themselves on their autonomy, should have taken their special character as much or more from the pressures of their environment as from their own inner desires; that institutions which identify themselves either as "private" or as "state" should have found their greatest stimulus in federal initiative; that universities which are part of a highly decentralized and varied system of higher education should, nevertheless, have responded with such fidelity and alacrity to national needs; that institutions which had their historical origins in the training of "gentlemen" should have committed themselves so fully to the service of brute technology.

The "federal grant" university has been emerging over the past twenty years, but until recently it has developed more by force of circumstances than by conscious design. The universities most affected have been making largely piecemeal adjustments to the new phenomena without any great effort at an overall view of what has been happening to them. Perhaps this was just as well—the transition probably was smoother precisely because it was not subjected to critical analysis. The federal government and the leading universities entered into a common-law marriage unblessed by predetermined policies and self-surveys—but nonetheless they formed a very productive union.

All this, however, as was inevitable, is being changed. Harvard has now studied itself. So has Princeton. Brookings and Carnegie have studied us all; so have the Department of Health, Education, and Welfare; the President's Science Advisory Committee; the American Council on Education; and the American Assembly.[2] The principal conclusion was predictable: the federal colossus had the power to influence the most ruggedly individual of universities. A paradox emerged: the better and the more individual the university, the greater its chances of succumbing to the federal embrace. Washington did not waste its money on the second-rate.

Soon there will be a national policy as well as nationwide activity, and I am at least a little concerned. All these studies have identified problems that we knew all along to exist. But now that we have publicly identified the problems, we shall be expected to deal with them; and in dealing with them we shall create new problems. Mostly, we shall have to strive for "balance" in a number of different ways. We shall have to "balance" the wishes of individual scholars with those of their institutions; New England with the South; the sciences with the humanities; research with teaching; graduate training with undergraduate education; merit with politics; the judgment of specialists with general formulae. And yet one of the more productive aspects of federal involvement to date has been its imbalance.

We are clearly entering the second phase of the "federal grant" development. The first I shall identify as the phase of "intuitive imbalance," and the new phase just emerging as one of "bureaucratic balance." It is a good time to examine where we have been and where we may be going. We are in the midst of a vast transformation of university life and none of us can be too sure where we really are going; but we can try to peer ahead.

As a basis for discussing the two phases of federal grant development, I shall briefly review the essential facts about federal involvement with universities in this country.

■ Federal interest in higher education dates from 1787. That year saw the beginning of endowment of public institutions of higher education with public lands, following the example of the Northwest Ordinance of 1785, which provided land to support public schools at the lower levels. However, this interest was not made effective until the Morrill Land Grant Act of 1862. Then the Second Morrill Act in 1890 supplemented the original land grants with federal grants of funds to support college instruction in specified subjects; these grants still continue, and, in fact, have recently been expanded. Federal interest in higher education was further made effective by the Hatch Act in 1887, establishing the Agricultural Experiment Stations, and by the Smith-Lever Act in 1914, creating the Agricultural Extension Service. During World War I, the ROTC program was established. During the Great Depression, universities were involved in the programs of the Work Projects Administration and National Youth Administration. During World War II, universities participated heavily in the Engineering, Science and Management War Training Program inaugurated in 1940. In that same year, the National Defense Research Committee (later the Office of Scientific Research and Development) was established, and leading universities became engaged in the various programs of war research it set up.

After World War II and again after the Korean conflict, the

"G.I. Bill" and the corresponding bill for Korean veterans sent a seismic shock through academic life.

Despite this long history of federal interest, however, it is evident that with the exception of the comparatively restricted areas of agriculture and military training, there was no continuing federal involvement with higher education until World War II.

■ Currently, federal support has become a major factor in the total performance of many universities, and the sums involved are substantial. Higher education in 1960 received about $1.5 billion from the federal government—a hundredfold increase in twenty years. About one third of this $1.5 billion was for university-affiliated research centers; about one third for project research within universities; and about one third for other things, such as residence hall loans, scholarships, and teaching programs. This last third was expended at colleges as well as universities, but the first two thirds almost exclusively at universities, and at relatively few of them.

The $1 billion for research, though only 10 percent of total federal support for research and development, accounted for 75 percent of all university expenditures on research and 15 percent of total university budgets. Clearly the shape and nature of university research are profoundly affected by federal monies.

■ Federal research funds to universities flow primarily from six agencies. In 1961 the percentage distribution was as follows:

Department of Health, Education, and Welfare (37
    percent was from National Institutes of Health
    alone) 39
Department of Defense 32
National Science Foundation. 11
Atomic Energy Commission 8
Department of Agriculture. 6
National Aeronautics and Space Administration 3
Other agencies 1

(These figures do not include funds for university-operated government research centers.)

This federal support has been almost exclusively identified with three great and somewhat interrelated national concerns: defense (40 percent of the total in 1961, including support by the Department of Defense and the Atomic Energy Commission); scientific and technological progress (20 percent—National Science Foundation, Department of Agriculture, and NASA); and health (37 percent—through the National Institutes of Health). Federal support has not been directed explicitly toward strengthening universities generally, or one or more universities specifically, in any over-all fashion—as might be said of the University Grants Committee in Great Britain.

▪ Federal research expenditures have been largely restricted to the physical and biomedical sciences, and engineering, with only about 3 percent for the social sciences and hardly any support for the humanities.

▪ Among the totality of university functions, federal support has been heavily concentrated on research and on graduate and postdoctoral training in fields of national interest.

▪ The preferred approach of the federal government to the use of university facilities for research has been (a) the specialized research center—by 1963 there were fourteen major ones,[3] and (b) the research project. Projects have been supported for relatively short terms and specific purposes; and support has been awarded, usually on the advice of qualified experts, on the basis of prospective performance.

▪ Federal research expenditures have been heavily focused on a relatively few institutions. If both project research and large research centers are included, six universities received 57 percent of the funds in a recent fiscal year, and twenty universities received 79 percent. If project research alone is considered, the figures are 28 and 54 percent. As a percentage of total university expenditures for all purposes among the leading twenty recipients, federal funds have amounted to 20 to 50 percent when project research alone is counted and from 20 to over 80 percent when the research centers are added. These twenty universities are only about one tenth of all universities in the United States. They constitute the primary federal grant universities.

 ▪ Recently there has been some spreading out of federal interest from the physical and biomedical to the social sciences; from graduate to undergraduate training; from a selective few to an expanded number of universities.

Phase One: Intuitive Imbalance

For about twenty years now, Congress has been deciding in which general areas the partnership between the federal government and the universities should be developed. The areas chosen have been defense, scientific and technological progress, and health. Decisions have not been based on thorough study of national priorities. They have been made pragmatically, in response to the felt needs of the nation and of the people in accord with the possibilities of the times, and also, to an extent, in response to the urgings of very powerful lobbies. The atom was split, and could be used for war and peace. The "cold war" followed World War II and necessitated further defense work. Health became a matter of great national concern. Possibilities for space exploration developed. Congress reacted quickly to each of these realities.

Once Congress initiated a program, federal administrative officers turned to those universities best able to give immediate and effective assistance on the individual programs; or rather they turned to those scientists in the best position to respond quickly and efficiently—and those scientists were principally located in a limited number of institutions. These actions were not undertaken on the basis of any general review of institutional capacity or potential capacity, but on quick and ready apprehension of possibilities and response to them. The test was who could most effectively do the job at hand. The process was more intuitive than studied.

For about twenty years, universities have been accepting the research centers and projects as proposed by faculty members and government agencies, making such day-to-day adjustments as were needed and possible. In consequence, these universities have been profoundly affected. The whole process has been one of starting new endeavors, and this has changed the pre-existing "balance" in several ways. Some real and some not so real issues have arisen for the universities.

1. *Federal control and federal influence.* Federal control as a substantive issue is, as Sidney Hook has said, a "red herring."[4] With a few exceptions—the generally necessary exception of secrecy in certain types of work and the unnecessary exception of the disclaimer affidavit required by the National Defense Education Act—there has been no control in any deleterious sense. By way of contrast, state control of state universities has been a real problem.[5] The federal government has customarily put scientifically trained persons in charge of science programs and they have operated fully within academic traditions.

The real problem is not one of federal control but of federal influence. A federal agency offers a project. A university need not accept—but, as a practical matter, it usually does. One of the quickest ways to lose a faculty member is by refusing to accept the grant he has just negotiated with his counterpart in Washington. Out of this reality have followed many of the consequences of federal aid for the universities; and they have been substantial. That they are subtle, slowly cumulative and gentlemanly makes them all the more potent.

2. *University control and the agency as alma mater.* A univer-

sity's control over its own destiny has been substantially reduced. University funds from tuition and fees, gifts and endowments, and state sources go through the usual budget-making procedures and their assignment is subject to review in accordance with internal policy. Federal research funds, however, are usually negotiated by the individual scholar with the particular agency, and so bypass the usual review process. Thus 20 to 50 to 80 percent of a university's expenditures may be handled outside the normal channels. These funds in turn commit some of the university's own funds; they influence the assignment of space; they determine the distribution of time between teaching and research; to a large extent they establish the areas in which the university grows the fastest. Almost imperceptibly, a university is changed.

The authority of the department chairman, the dean, the president is thereby reduced; so also is the role of faculty government. This may have its advantages. Scholars seem to prefer dealing with their professional counterparts in Washington rather than with their colleagues and administrators at home.[6] Also the university's internal process of distributing funds would be generally less selective and less flexible than the federal research project approach. Within a university, the tendency is to give each faculty member about the same opportunity and once having given it to keep giving it thereafter; but the project method allows more attention to exceptional merit and has the advantage that all projects may end some time. Additionally, federal agencies are more responsive to particular national needs than the universities would be, given the same amount of money to spend according to their own priority system.

There are, however, clearly detrimental effects. Some faculty members come to use the pressure of their agency contacts against their university. They may try to force the establishment of a new administrative unit or the assignment of land for their own special building, in defiance of general university policy or priorities. These pressures, of course, should be withstood; they speak well neither of the professor nor of the agency. Also, some faculty members tend to shift their identification and loyalty from their university to the agency in Washington. Their concern with the general welfare of the university is eroded and they become tenants rather than owners, taking their grants with them as they change their institutional lodgings. The university, as Allen Wallis, president of the University of Rochester, has remarked, becomes to an extent a "hotel." The agency becomes the new alma mater. The research entrepreneur becomes a euphoric schizophrenic.

It has been said that, in the face of federal aid, university presidents have "abdicated" their responsibilities for the general conduct of their institutions. I would put it differently—they have let some things go by that they would have liked to do differently; but this is often what they do anyway. There are, however, especially acute problems when the agency insists on the tie-in sale (if we do this for you, then you must do that for us) or when it requires frequent and detailed progress reports. Then the university really is less than a free agent. It all becomes a kind of "putting-out" system with the agency taking the place of the merchant-capitalist of old. Sweat shops have developed out of such a system in earlier times and in other industries.

3. *"Scientists Affluent, Humanists Militant."*[7] Federal research support has added a new dimension to the eternal class struggles within a university. To student versus faculty, assistant versus tenured professors, and faculty versus administrators has been added a new hierarchical point of tension—that between humanists and scientists. The scientists, by and large, in the federal grant universities, get promoted faster, get more space, get more

income through summer employment and consulting, have more secretaries and assistants, have greater access to travel funds and expense accounts, and accumulate a greater sense of status within and outside the academic community. Some humanists obviously resent all this and consider it quite unfair, even though their own situation has improved, relative to what it used to be.

However, there is still another side to the story. The scientist who gets a series of projects going can become caught in his own apparatus. Graduate students and staff members become dependent upon him. He is committed to project deadlines and periodic contract negotiations. He is enmeshed in a web of obligations and it is very hard to break out. As a result, he often works hard at things he would rather not do—more often than need be true of the humanist.

There is some current tendency for the brightest of graduate students to prefer the sciences to the social sciences and the humanities,[8] and this will have an impact on comparative faculty quality as between fields of study in the years to come. How much of this has been caused by federal aid and how much by the current liveliness of the different fields is not at all clear. My own impression is that the brightest graduate students flock to the areas with the brightest new ideas, regardless of federal aid.

All this is said to have destroyed the "balance" among fields and it is generally concluded that something should be done about it. The balance among fields, however, has never been a static thing. If it were, philosophy, theology, and the classics would still be the dominant areas of study, as they have not been for a long time. Assuming that the balance of 1942, say, was appropriate for 1942, this does not mean it would have been appropriate for 1962. It is not enough to say that the old "balance" has been destroyed. The real question is what should be the proper balance today? It is clear that the flowering of the

Renaissance should have affected the "balance" in the sixteenth century. It would seem likely that the splitting of the atom and the deciphering of the genetic code should in their turn affect the balance of the twentieth century. We should expect the most money and the brightest students and the greatest prestige to follow the most exciting new ideas. By and large they have done so, and this is one way of defining the nature of balance. (Economics was exciting in the 1930's; sociology was more exciting in the 1950's.)

The real question, it seems to me, is not one of balance in any historical or monetary sense, but rather what is most appropriate to each field in each period. "All fields are equal, only some are more equal than others." There should be no effort to do the same things in the same amounts for each field. Each should receive support in accordance with its current potentialities, and potentialities vary. There are no timeless priorities.

The academic community has lived with inequities before. Agriculture in the land grant institutions has had eleven-month appointments, low teaching loads, and heavy research subsidies for decades. Law and medicine have reflected within the academic world some of the power and affluence of their professions in the outside world. These are stated as matters of fact, not as ideal situations.

Generally, I think, it is remarkable and commendable that so high a degree of internal equity has thus far been preserved within the academic world in the face of quite chaotic pressures impinging upon it.

4. *The inevitability of concentration.* The project approach almost automatically led to concentration of federal research effort in a relatively few universities. The universities best equipped to undertake the research were also those with the faculty and facilities to provide for the training of Ph.D.'s. It is no coinci-

dence that the six universities with a little more than 25 percent of project funds graduated about 25 percent of the Ph.D.'s; and a similar situation prevails for the top twenty universities. If "only the best will do,"[9] this concentration of effort is inevitable. A different result would have been quite surprising.

This concentration of effort has undoubtedly strengthened the facilities and improved the quality of faculties of universities already in the front rank. It has probably widened the gap between those of the first and those of the second and third ranks. It may, in fact, have actually injured universities of the second and third ranks and some colleges by turning their potential faculty members into research personnel in the front-rank universities. The good are better; the poor may well be worse. And it has greatly accentuated the differences between colleges and universities.

5. *Teaching the graduates versus teaching the undergraduates.* The much-advertised conflict between teaching and research puts the problem the wrong way. The teaching of graduate students is so closely tied to research that if research is improved, graduate instruction is almost bound to be improved also. And the almost universal experience seems to be that federal research support has improved graduate instruction. There have been better facilities, more research assistantships and fellowships, more research projects in which students can work directly with faculty members—all resulting from federal funds. At the graduate level, there has been a clear gain, and fortunately so, because graduate enrollments at the federal grant universities have been increasing rapidly.

At the undergraduate level, however, the "subtle discounting of the teaching process"[10] has been aided and abetted. Harold Orlans, who conducted the excellent Brookings study of federal aid to universities, concludes that federal research aid "has accelerated the long-standing depreciation of undergraduate education at large universities."[11] This is my own observation, with one exception—that a very few private institutions with long traditions of very high-quality undergraduate instruction have been able to maintain their standards; and this is to their great credit.

The reasons for the general deterioration of undergraduate teaching are several. Teaching loads and student contact hours have been reduced. Faculty members are more frequently on leave or temporarily away from the campus; some are never more than temporarily on campus. More of the instruction falls to teachers who are not members of the regular faculty. The best graduate students prefer fellowships and research assistantships to teaching assistantships. Postdoctoral fellows who might fill the gap usually do not teach. Average class size has been increasing.

There seems to be a "point of no return" after which research, consulting, graduate instruction become so absorbing that faculty efforts can no longer be concentrated on undergraduate instruction as they once were. This process has been going on for a long time; federal research funds have intensified it. As a consequence, undergraduate education in the large university is more likely to be acceptable than outstanding; educational policy from the undergraduate point of view is largely neglected. How to escape the cruel paradox that a superior faculty results in an inferior concern for undergraduate teaching is one of our more pressing problems.

6. *The faculty and the un-faculty.* University scholars traditionally have both taught and conducted research. But now some scholars are added to the staff in exclusively research capacities—and increasingly with titles suggesting professorial status. They have no teaching responsibilities and are not as yet fully accepted members of the academic community. They usually are

not members of the Academic Senate and they usually are not given tenure—both traditional marks of faculty status. In many institutions, however, they may use the name of the university in getting projects under their own direction.

In a far less anomalous position is the faculty member who works on a federally sponsored project during the summer months and part-time during the regular year, and receives much of his pay from the project rather than from the university. But to what extent is he really a university employee and what security of employment does he really have? Obviously, it is no longer so clear as it once was just who is the faculty.

There has been an almost frantic remaking of the rules—new titles created, new relationships established, new classes of citizenship formulated and only partially assimilated. The Harvard catalogue now lists more than 5,000 "Officers of Instruction and Administration," many of whom are not faculty in the traditional sense. The "faculty" in our universities becomes an ever-changing group as the definitions change. If there can still be said to be a "faculty" at all, it is most certainly a different composite than before. Much of the teaching, much of the research is done by the "un-faculty."

7. *University "aid" to the federal government.* Federal aid has been of great benefit to the universities. It has not, however, been without its costs in money and effort. Overhead allowances vary greatly from agency to agency but seldom cover all the indirect as well as the direct costs of sponsored research. Also, matching grants for construction may force a university to upset its own priority system in order to get federal funds. This, of course, is the intent.

Additionally, federal funds have placed great new administrative burdens on the universities—on faculty members, on department chairmen, on deans, on presidents. New classes of administrators have been created—the contracting officer and the research project manager. Administration becomes a much larger aspect of the total university enterprise. Julius A. Stratton has observed, "There is a basic incompatibility between the true spirit of a university and those elements of management which tend to creep into the organization of projects, the planning of programs, and the utilization of costly facilities."[12]

8. *On the borders of temptation.* Immense sums of money have been poured into the universities by the federal government, and universities are highly atomistic entities. The university has the responsibility for but usually not the actual control of these funds. Some abuses have inevitably developed. Funds have been diverted at times from one use to another—and the other a use not intended by the federal agency. Some faculty members make informal alliances—if you consult on my project, then I should consult on yours—and total income has been pyramided through this exchange of consultancies to occasionally astounding levels. When these same faculty members sit on the federal panels that make the grants, the whole process becomes quite involved, to say the least. Excessive amounts of expensive equipment have at times been purchased, and equipment salesmen chase grants around. Some universities promise not only a base salary but substantial supplemental personal income and allowances from federal grants as a recruiting device in a wilder and wilder upward spiral.

There have been some scandals. There will be more. The federal agencies will exercise increasingly specific controls and the universities dependent on this new standard of living will accept these controls. The universities themselves will have to exercise more stringent controls by centralizing authority, particularly through the audit process. In a few situations, self-restraint has not been enough restraint; as one result, greater external restraint will be imposed in most situations.

With all its problems, however, federal research aid to universities has helped greatly in meeting national needs. It has greatly assisted the universities themselves. The nation is stronger. The leading universities are stronger. As Nathan Pusey reported the unanimous views of the presidents of universities participating in the Carnegie study, federal aid, over all, has been a "good thing."[13] In their turn, the federal grant universities have adapted to their new role quite quickly and effectively.

Professor Don Price has made reference to the following limerick:

> There was a young lady from Kent
> Who said that she knew what it meant
>   When men took her to dine,
>   Gave her cocktails and wine;
> She knew what it meant—but she went.[14]

I am not so sure that the universities and their presidents always knew what it meant; but one thing is certain—they went.

Phase Two: Bureaucratic Balance

The general policy of federal agencies in allocating research grants to universities for the last two decades has been one of "seeking excellence wherever it is," one of accepting the established pattern and following it. The new approach is to take more of an over-all view; to change the pattern to a degree. Balance is the new virtue; imbalance the old sin.

The charge, made by Logan Wilson among others, has been that "There is no federal program—merely programs."[15] The response—in the proposed "National Education Improvement Act of 1963," for example—is to provide: "A comprehensive program of Federal aid to meet selected and urgent needs of American education on all levels from elementary school through

graduate education; to promote educational quality, expand opportunity for education, and to increase the capacity of our
educational institutions; to provide for the Nation's needs in
skilled manpower, national growth, and national security."

The new balance calls for developing a larger number of
outstanding centers of graduate instruction and research. The
Seaborg report suggested an expansion from the present fifteen
or twenty centers to thirty or forty over a fifteen-year period.[16]
The National Education Improvement Act envisages expansion
from twenty to seventy. This demand for geographical dispersion
of centers of strength follows, in part, the new realization of the
role of a university as a factor influencing the location of industry. The Roswell L. Gilpatric report for the Department of Defense explained the concentration of defense contracts in California and Massachusetts by the concentration of research and
development projects in these two states, which in turn was
attributed to the availability of university centers of substantial
strength.[17] An educational and political effort of considerable
dimensions now seeks to reorder the current pattern of distribution in the name of balance.

Under the National Defense Education Act of 1958, preference
is already given to assisting *new* graduate programs in selected
subject matter areas. Teaching is being emphasized along with
research. Summer refresher courses for teachers of science, improvement of science textbooks, and language laboratories are
programs already well established. The National Science Foundation has a large effort under way to improve and renovate
equipment for undergraduate teaching in the physical sciences.
Undergraduates, as well as graduate students, are being assisted
by loans and scholarships. The social sciences are receiving increasing sums of money. More funds are being granted to colleges
as well as to universities, and to universities of all ranks. In

particular, "institutional grants," to supplement project grants, are being given by the National Science Foundation and the National Institutes of Health. And NASA, among others, makes "training" grants to institutions instead of awarding fellowships to students who may then go wherever they wish. Thus, efforts to achieve greater "balance" are already well under way.

The approach to a university "as an institution" is of particular interest. If additional universities are to be selected to become centers of strength in research and graduate instruction, then it will be necessary for the federal government to be concerned with the "general health of the institution." This will be a notable departure from historical practice, except in agriculture. The Land Grant Association, in commenting on recent recommendations by the President's Science Advisory Committee for dispersion through assistance to institutions as such, said: "The recommendations represent a return to the principles of government-institution relations laid down in the basic land grant legislation, in which the responsibility for internal administration, fiscal management, and proper direction is vested with university officers rather than with agency staffs."[18] It should be noted that *every* state has at least one land grant institution receiving federal support on a formula basis. The parallel with agriculture is not entirely apt, however, since agriculture by its very nature is locally and regionally oriented, but national defense and space exploration are not.

If we are to move toward federal orientation to the "total function of the university," then the University Grants Committee in Great Britain is the outstanding precedent, and one that has received some support in the United States.[19] However, there are only about thirty universities in Great Britain and it is clear what is and what is not a university. Additionally, the University Grants Committee has come to exercise more influence over the establishment of new programs, the cost and size and even the appearance of new buildings, the equalization of faculty salaries among institutions, and the determination of admission policies than would currently be acceptable if it came from the federal government in this country.

Some hard choices must be faced. The decentralized project approach of the last two decades has much to recommend it. It is selective on merit, flexible in accordance with quality of performance, and responsive to national goals. The universities and their scholars retain substantial freedom. But such dominant reliance on the project approach is no longer likely. In fact, the project is already less the chosen instrument than it once was. Productive anarchy is no longer such a politically viable solution.

It is said that support to institutions as such will "give a university the necessary autonomy," and will permit dispersion of effort and better balance in several directions. It is not clear, however, how the particular institutions will be chosen, or, once chosen, how support might subsequently be withdrawn if performance should prove inadequate. It is difficult to assess the merit of a total institution as complex as a modern university. One alternative is to rely on a formula, as in the case of agriculture in the land grant institutions. Another is to be guided by political influence; and this is increasingly happening.

It is reported that Congress already senses its loss of control to the professional personnel in the various agencies and would like to regain it. "Congress knows it has forfeited much power over science to the Executive and it does not like it."[20] The Harvard self-study report notes the danger of political interference and "log-rolling" inherent in block grants.[21] Inter-university competition would be taken from the quasi-academic arena of the agency committee to the legislative halls.

Additionally, the selection of designated "centers of strength" assumes a single source of designation—a single over-all federal agency or committee. A single agency means a single source of control, as against the current pluralistic situation of several agencies and several sources of influence, with opportunity to pick and choose among them. A single source of control would turn an influential relationship into a really "perilous partnership."[22] Finally, will funds necessarily be better spent for the national interest under institutional control than through the agencies, where decisions are freer from internal rigidities and egalitarian tendencies?

In the battle over institutional versus project support, Congressmen are more likely to prefer the institutional approach than are the professionals in the agencies; the presidents of universities than the researchers within the universities; the less well-established universities than the well-established ones; the humanists than the scientists—generally, those who have less under the project system than those who have more.

It is almost obligatory in educational circles these days to support "excellence" *and* "balance." They are the two magic words. Yet "excellence" and "balance" sometimes pull in different directions. It is also quite necessary to favor "institutional integrity" and to be against "federal control." Yet the institutional grants that aid what we are supposed to favor (integrity) may also aid what we are supposed to be against (control). Turning "integrity" over to the university president may also turn "control" over to the federal government.

How can we really best secure "aristocracy of achievement arising out of democracy of opportunity?"[23]

Some Suggestions

The nation does face some grave problems in the field of education. Vastly increased numbers of students are pouring into our schools. Many qualitative deficiencies exist. State and local subdivisions are caught with relatively fixed tax structures, and private endowments and gifts have their limits also. Federal support is the most obvious way out. But federal expenditures themselves are not unlimited, and there are some realistic barriers to certain types of federal involvement.

The first consideration is that the federal government need not and cannot do everything. It seems to me that the educational system of America, good as it generally is, is in the most trouble—and thus in the greatest need of federal help—at the bottom and at the top.

At the bottom is the problem of "drop-outs" from school and "drop-outs" of the unskilled from the employed labor force. Through occupational training and retraining, through counseling, guidance, and relocation, these "drop-outs" should be assisted to acquire skills valuable in a dynamic economy where skill levels are rising at perhaps the fastest rate in history. Full employment is the necessary complement to make such training effective.

At the top, the nation needs more research activity in a number of fields and more personnel of high skill—particularly engineers, scientists, mathematicians, teachers, and medical doctors. A recent Bureau of Labor Statistics survey shows that from now to 1970 the expected supply of engineers and scientists will fill only three quarters of the demand. This leaves a very large gap. The prospect is particularly critical for engineers.

Fortunately the levels where federal aid is most necessary are levels where it is most politically feasible. My suggestions will be limited to higher education, and to the university level in particular.

1. Federal research centers, whenever possible, should be located near and identified with a university. A university, with its libraries, colleagues to talk to, and graduate students to train,

provides a uniquely favorable environment for such centers. In turn, such centers provide additional research opportunities for the university's faculty members and graduate students. Instead of establishing a research center in isolation and then, perhaps, having to build a new university at the same site, it seems to me best to put the center near some university—even if it doesn't happen to be our own.

2. The project system should be continued in essentially its present form as the major means of supporting the research and graduate instruction programs of universities as well as accomplishing the specific research purposes of the federal government. If project funds double or triple during the decade of the sixties, as now seems likely, it will be possible and necessary to extend more of them beyond the twenty institutions that constitute the primary group of federal grant universities at the present time. Orlans has identified about ten universities, mostly "public" ones, which already deserve considerably more project support on the basis of their existing Ph.D. programs.[24] Other universities will soon be moving into this group in the natural course of events. The project system follows established lines of contact through disciplines and avoids the problems of establishing a new reliance on institutional lines of contact.

The project system has resulted in a "highly successful working relationship between the government's need for long- and short-term research and the academic scientist's abilities and interests."[25]

To the extent that institutional grants are given, they should follow the project grants. Charles V. Kidd has suggested that 25 percent might be given as free funds to institutions, as against 75 percent in project funds.[26] Twenty-five percent appears to be an adequate figure. These institutional grants could best be used by the universities for new projects, small projects, support of young faculty members unknown in Washington, and of fields neglected in direct federal grants—all on a very flexible basis. Thus the universities' rather different evaluation of "merit" could supplement the standards for merit of the federal agencies. I would hope that the institutional grants would be assigned automatically by the agencies as some percentage of the project grants which are themselves assigned on merit. If "quality must come first,"[27] this is the best way to assure it.

Alvin M. Weinberg has recently made the interesting suggestion that the panel system of reviewing research proposals could be improved as an instrument for making scientific judgments by including on the panels representatives of related fields, as well as representatives of the field in question. "I should think that advice from panels so constituted," he says, "would be tempered by concern for larger issues; in particular the support of a proposed research project would be viewed from the larger perspective of the relevance of that research to the rest of science."[28] The greater impartiality of the panels would also be assured.

Contract and grant overhead should cover reasonable indirect as well as all direct costs.

Federal project funds are increasingly being used to bid salaries and allowances up and to bid teaching assignments down. How much further such competition can go without raising grave policy problems for the federal agencies is problematical. The market is sufficiently active without this added inflationary stimulus; and the universities are sufficiently in trouble with internal inequities and reduction of teaching time.

There is currently arising a three-sided competitive struggle for research and development work, involving industry, the universities, and the government itself.[29] The universities should be preferred for basic research and for such other research as is readily related to graduate instruction.

It is being suggested, and also being implemented, that federal grants and contracts be channeled increasingly into liberal arts colleges to assist faculty research and the training of outstanding undergraduate students. This process can easily subvert the colleges from their primary obligation and start them on the way to becoming quite different types of institutions. With a project-by-project approach this is almost bound to happen. Would it not be well for the governing bodies of such colleges to examine the implications of this changed role before the process of project-by-project transformation of the nature of the institution is begun? If they accept the role they should accept it by a conscious policy decision.

3. To aid the teaching function of universities during the "deficit years" of greatly swollen enrollments just ahead, federal agencies should permit, even encourage, postdoctoral fellows and research professors to teach one-quarter or even one-third time at no cost to the institution. The present system increases the size of the "un-faculty" and widens the gap between the researcher and the student. Also, the further creation of research career professorships might well be examined. Are they really necessary from a research point of view and is it really desirable to preclude their occupants from normal participation in the full range of academic life?

The universities themselves should see to it that teaching assistantships are fully competitive with research assistantships and fellowships.

4. Federal agencies should provide space and equipment for their postdoctoral fellows and research career professors and for all contracts and most grants without the requirement of matching funds. It is very difficult to obtain space and equipment for these purposes from either endowments or state support, and also not entirely appropriate.

5. A National Foundation for Higher Education might well

be created on the model of the National Science Foundation. It could serve as a focal point for the interests of higher education and make grants outside the province of the National Science Foundation. Such a foundation would need to explore carefully the areas where support would be most productive, and also the appropriate forms of support, as did the National Science Foundation with such skill and judgment in its fields of interest. Areas for possible early consideration, as examples, are the creative arts, international studies, and environmental planning. Each is at a stage of considerable activity; each carries a high degree of national interest. Additionally, a Foundation for Higher Education might well undertake the support of great regional library resources with union catalogues made available to other university and college libraries in the region.

6. A number of other federal programs now in effect to aid higher education have generally worked well and should be continued.

The established program of the Federal Housing Authority in making loans for residence halls, student unions, and parking structures should be continued and expanded, as should the several programs under the National Defense Education Act. These programs are all widely dispersed in their efforts, and affect nearly all universities and many colleges.

Graduate fellowship programs should be expanded as there are capable graduate students to fill them. The availability of money does not by itself create a supply of competent candidates. At least half of the graduate fellowships should be transferable on a national basis, and not more than half tied to particular institutions. The practice of the Rockefeller Foundation and Woodrow Wilson Foundation of making an institutional grant to cover part of the institutional expenses for each scholar might well be more widely emulated.

The great need for curriculum reform in many fields, caused by the changing content and structure of knowledge growing out of research, should be recognized by federal agencies. They should support the efforts of universities to re-examine and improve the teaching in these areas. Some support is being given, particularly by the National Science Foundation in the physical sciences, but unfortunately some recent developments run counter to this trend. For example, the National Institutes of Health now cannot support any such efforts in the biological sciences—an area where they are greatly needed.

Foreign service projects conducted by universities for the federal government appear to be most fruitful if there is a major institutional assignment for a substantial period of time. *Ad hoc* projects accomplish little for the foreign country or for the contracting university.

7. Medical and dental doctors are in short supply and will be in shorter supply. Fellowships and facilities for their training deserve high federal priority.[30]

8. A Council of Advisers on Education, as suggested by the American Assembly in 1960,[31] would provide an opportunity for an over-all view of the educational system and the educational needs of the nation as no single agency can do. This would be something like the President's Council of Economic Advisers, but in the educational field. Education may well need a better-coordinated voice than it has had, as McGeorge Bundy has so eloquently argued,[32] but the federal government also may need a more coordinated ear.

This council might assist in the preparation of a manpower budget covering the supply of, and demand for, the skills that depend on formal education. Indeed, beyond this the nation might benefit from an over-all manpower budget, supplementing its other budgets, for it would focus attention on human resources and on the importance of developing them.

The partnership of the federal government with higher education and particularly with the federal grant universities over the last two decades has been enormously productive in enlarging the pool of scientific ideas and skills. Now we are entering a new phase of widening and deepening relationships. This new phase can carry the American commitment to education to new heights of endeavor. It can also preserve the traditional freedom of higher education from excessive control. It can enlarge the horizons of equality of opportunity. It can maintain and even increase the margin for excellence. The challenge is to make certain it does all these things.

3

THE FUTURE OF THE CITY
OF INTELLECT

"The true American University,"
David Starr Jordan once observed, "lies in the future." It still
does; for American universities have not yet developed their full
identity, their unique theory of purpose and function. They still
look to older and to foreign models, although less and less; and
the day is coming when these models will no longer serve at all.

The task of prophecy is made difficult by the many internal
and external cross-currents to which universities are exposed.
Archibald MacLeish wrote in 1941: "Like other private institutions, Harvard must face the fact that gifts to the university in
the foreseeable future will not equal in bulk the gifts of the late
twenties. Like other private institutions, it must admit that the
peak of enrollment has probably been reached. And like other
private institutions it must therefore accept the fact that this
period of its history will be a period of organization within
existing frontiers, rather than a period of extension of existing
frontiers."[1] Since 1941 Harvard has become a federal grant
university, has obtained private gifts beyond previous experience,

has expanded far beyond its then "existing frontiers." This illustration serves to demonstrate that prophecy has its perils when treating with as dynamic an institution in as changing an environment as the modern American university.

The Second Transformation

The American university is currently undergoing its second great transformation. The first occurred during roughly the last quarter of the nineteenth century, when the land grant movement and German intellectualism were together bringing extraordinary change. The current transformation will cover roughly the quarter century after World War II. The university is being called upon to educate previously unimagined numbers of students; to respond to the expanding claims of national service; to merge its activities with industry as never before; to adapt to and rechannel new intellectual currents. By the end of this period, there will be a truly American university, an institution unique in world history, an institution not looking to other models but serving, itself, as a model for universities in other parts of the globe. This is not said in boast. It is simply that the imperatives that have molded the American university are at work around the world.

Each nation, as it has become influential, has tended to develop the leading intellectual institutions of its world—Greece, the Italian cities, France, Spain, England, Germany, and now the United States. The great universities have developed in the great periods of the great political entities of history. Today, more than ever, education is inextricably involved in the quality of a nation. It has been estimated that over the last thirty years nearly half of our national growth can be explained by the greater education of our people and by better technology, which is also largely a product of the educational system.[2]

So many of the hopes and fears of the American people are now related to our educational system and particularly to our universities—the hope for longer life, for getting into outer space, for a higher standard of living; our fears of Russian or Chinese supremacy, of the bomb and annihilation, of individual loss of purpose in the changing world. For all these reasons and others, the university has become a prime instrument of national purpose. This is new. This is the essence of the transformation now engulfing our universities.

The knowledge industry.   Basic to this transformation is the growth of the "knowledge industry," which is coming to permeate government and business and to draw into it more and more people raised to higher and higher levels of skill. The production, distribution, and consumption of "knowledge" in all its forms is said to account for 29 percent of gross national product, according to Fritz Machlup's calculations; and "knowledge production" is growing at about twice the rate of the rest of the economy.[3] Knowledge has certainly never in history been so central to the conduct of an entire society. What the railroads did for the second half of the last century and the automobile for the first half of this century may be done for the second half of this century by the knowledge industry: that is, to serve as the focal point for national growth. And the university is at the center of the knowledge process.

The university historically has been growing in concentric circles. It started with philosophy in Greece, and a library—the first great one—at Alexandria. It spread to the ancient professions, and then to science. It permeated agriculture and now industry. Originally it served the elites of society, then the middle class as well, and now it includes the children of all, regardless of social and economic background.

Spatially the modern university often reflects its history, with the library and the humanities and social sciences at the center of the campus, extending out to the professional schools and scientific laboratories, and surrounded by industry, interspersed with residence halls, apartments, and boarding houses. An almost ideal location for a modern university is to be sandwiched between a middle-class district on its way to becoming a slum and an ultramodern industrial park—so that the students may live in the one and the faculty consult in the other. M.I.T. finds itself happily ensconced between the decaying sections of Cambridge and Technology Square.

Universities have become "bait" to be dangled in front of industry, with drawing power greater than low taxes or cheap labor. Route 128 around Boston and the great developing industrial complexes in the San Francisco Bay Area and Southern California reflect the universities in these areas. The Gilpatric report for the Department of Defense explained that 41 percent of defense contracts for research in the fiscal year 1961 were concentrated in California, 12 percent in New York, and 6 percent in Massachusetts, for a total of nearly 60 percent, in part because these were also "centers of learning."[4] Sterling Forest outside New York City seeks to attract industry by location next to a new university campus.[5] In California, new industrial laboratories were located next to two new university campuses before the first building was built on either of these campuses.

Sometimes industry will reach into a university laboratory to extract the newest ideas almost before they are born. Instead of waiting outside the gates, agents are working the corridors. They also work the placement offices. And the university, in turn, reaches into industry, as through the Stanford Research Institute.

The new connection of the university with the rise and fall of industrial areas has brought about an inter-university and inter-regional competition unmatched in history except by the universities and their *Länder* in nineteenth-century Germany. Texas and Pittsburgh seek to imitate what California and Boston have known; so also do Iowa, Seattle, and nearly all the rest. A vast campaign is on to see that the university center of each industrial complex shall not be "second best."

It is often through new academic specialties and through athletics that the universities seeking to rise in the academic hierarchy can most quickly and easily attract national attention—and also by hiring great and visible academic stars. The mark of a university "on the make" is a mad scramble for football stars and professorial luminaries. The former do little studying and the latter little teaching, and so they form a neat combination of muscle and intellect.

The university and segments of industry are becoming more alike. As the university becomes tied into the world of work, the professor—at least in the natural and some of the social sciences—takes on the characteristics of an entrepreneur. Industry, with its scientists and technicians, learns an uncomfortable bit about academic freedom and the handling of intellectual personnel. The two worlds are merging physically and psychologically.

The rise of Ideopolis.   University centers have a tendency to coalesce. Allan Nevins has put it this way: "Observers of higher education can now foresee the inexorable emergence of an entirely new landscape. It will no longer show us a nation dotted by high academic peaks with lesser hills between; it will be a landscape dominated by mountain ranges."[6] The highest peaks of the future will rise from the highest plateaus.

One such plateau runs from Boston to Washington. At the universities and laboratories situated along this range are found 46 percent of the American Nobel Prize winners in the sciences and 40 percent of the members of the National Academy of Sciences. A second range with its peaks runs along the California

coast. C. P. Snow has written: "And now the scientific achievement of the United States is moving at a rate we all ought to
marvel at. Think of the astonishing constellation of talent, particularly in the physical sciences, all down the California coast,
from Berkeley and Stanford to Pasadena and Los Angeles. There
is nothing like that concentration of talent anywhere in the
world. It sometimes surprises Europeans to realize how much of
the pure science of the entire West is being carried out in the
United States. Curiously enough, it often surprises Americans
too. At a guess, the figure is something like 80 percent, and might
easily be higher."[7]

The California mountain range has 36 percent of the Nobel
laureates in science and 20 percent of the members of the National Academy of Sciences. The Big Ten and Chicago constitute
a third range of academic peaks, with 10 percent of the Nobel
laureates and 14 percent of the members of the National Academy of Sciences. These three groupings of universities—the East
Coast, California, and the Big Ten and Chicago—currently produce over three quarters of the doctorates conferred in the United
States. Another range may be in the process of development in
the Texas-Louisiana area.

This concentration of talent partly follows history—the location of the older private and public universities. Partly it follows
industrial strengths and population centers. But it also has its
own logic. No one university can cover all specialties, or cover
them well enough so that there is a sufficient cluster of close
intellectual colleagues. The scholar dislikes intellectual isolation
and good scholars tend to swarm together. These swarms are
extraordinarily productive environments. No library can be complete; nor any graduate curriculum. Some laboratories, to be well
used, must be used by more than one university. Thus the Big
Ten and Chicago, through their Committee on Institutional Co-

operation, are merging their library resources, creating a "common market" for graduate students, diversifying their research laboratories on a common-use basis, and parceling out foreign language specializations. Something similar is happening in the University of California system, and between Berkeley and Stanford. Harvard and M.I.T., Princeton and Pennsylvania, among others, run joint research enterprises.

These clustering universities, in turn, have clustering around them scientifically oriented industrial and governmental enterprises. To match the drawing power of the great metropolis, there now arrives the new Ideopolis. The isolated mountain can no longer dominate the landscape; the constellation is greater than the single star and adds to the brightness of the sky.

There are other possible patterns for development. France and Russia have not made their universities so central to the life of society. They have segregated their research institutes to a substantial degree and established separate institutions for much of their technical training. Also, both have set up their universities on a regional basis with one university having a monopoly in the region. Both France and Russia, however, are now making their universities more central mechanisms, and Paris and Moscow, in particular, are the dominating institutions. Nevertheless, their basic pattern is quite different from the American, and, I think, not as productive.

With these national, industrial, and academic pulls upon them, universities need to be quickly responsive to opportunities, readily adaptable to change. Yet they are basically conservative institutions. Jacques Barzun in his *House of Intellect* presents this "House" from an inward looking and idealistic point of view, as one opposed to the "corruption" of science, to modern art, to foundations with their interdisciplinary projects, and so forth, regretting that the "House" is no longer "a company apart."[8]

However, the "City of Intellect" of the modern university also must look outward and to reality; it cannot be "a company apart." This conflict between internal and external dynamics has always been a difficult one for universities but never so intense as at present when the imperatives of change press so unmercifully against the necessities of internal harmony.

Conservative Institutions—Dynamic Environment

There are two great clichés about the university. One pictures it as a radical institution, when in fact it is most conservative in its institutional conduct. The other pictures it as autonomous, a cloister, when the historical fact is that it has always responded, but seldom so quickly as today, to the desires and demands of external groups—sometimes for love, sometimes for gain, increasingly willingly, and, in some cases, too eagerly. The external view is that the university is radical; the internal reality is that it is conservative. The internal illusion is that it is a law unto itself; the external reality is that it is governed by history.

The university's gate of Janus leads inward as well as outward, and inside the gate the social landscape changes remarkably. When one looks inward toward the "ivory tower," he sees a different "looking-glass land." Here, to get somewhere, you must run twice as slowly. This is as it must be. The university, as an institution, needs to create an environment that gives to its faculty members:

a sense of stability—they should not fear constant change that distracts them from their work;

a sense of security—they should not need to worry about the attacks against them from outside the gate;

a sense of continuity—they should not be concerned that their work and the structure of their lives will be greatly disrupted;

a sense of equity—they should not be suspicious that others are being treated better than they are.

Inventiveness should be left to the individual faculty member within the protection and solidity of the surrounding institutional structure. Galileo within the conservative institution of Padua in his day, Erasmus at Oxford and Freiburg, Newton at Cambridge helped start the enormous metamorphosis from which the modern world emerged. But their institutions, as institutions, were stolidly changeless.

The faculty guild.   "Nothing should ever be done for the first time" was the wry conclusion of F. M. Cornford from his vantage point as a classicist at Cambridge University at the turn of the century when Cambridge was stirring with responses to the modern world. He added that "Nothing is ever done until every one is convinced that it ought to be done, and has been convinced for so long that it is now time to do something else."[9] John Stuart Mill had looked upon the British universities of his day as largely unrelated to the progress of national life. Harold Laski, a century after Mill, felt that Oxford and Cambridge operated under a form of "syndicalism," which he considered the antithesis of the social usefulness he sought, and that they were only partly saved by being shaken up by royal commissions every thirty or forty years. Flexner referred to universities generally as "institutions usually regarded as conservative, frequently even as strongholds of reaction," and added that "institutions as such tend for quite obvious reasons to lag behind the life which they express and further."[10]

With reference to the American scene, Frederick Rudolph in his recent authoritative study of American colleges and universities concluded that "Resistance to fundamental reform was ingrained in the American collegiate and university tradition, as over three hundred years of history demonstrated. . . . Except on rare occasions, the historic policy of the American college and university [was]: drift, reluctant accommodation, belated recognition that while no one was looking, change had in fact taken place."[11] Nevitt Sanford, after a study of more contemporary focus, observed that there have been few innovations at all and even fewer "initiated by college or university faculties"; when a movement for reform has come, "it is the collective faculty who usually seem to be dragging their feet."[12]

There is a kind of "guild mentality" in the academic profession, as in many others. The guild was isolationist toward society, devoted to producer as against consumer sovereignty, and committed more to guild rules than to quick adaptation to popular demand. The guild was egalitarian, full of senatorial courtesy, selective of its own members. It was also a "sort of club" as Snow has characterized the colleges of Cambridge and Oxford,[13] and an "oligarchy of senior professors" as Ashby has noted about these same institutions.[14] In Germany, the faculty was more a class structure than a guild—a class structure intimately tied into the class structure of the surrounding society, hierarchical rather than fraternal.

The self-contained guild idea is still an attractive ideal. One recent call to faculty members is to "close our gates," become "masters within our walls," assume a "posture of offence" against the surrounding society.[15] Yet, except in a few situations, the faculty guild has never been a fully self-governing guild in reality, and almost never a company of "free agents,"[16] much as it might like to believe itself one. However, the guild idea, the "Republic of Scholars," is often and understandably the faculty member's vision of "pie-in-the-sky."

Some of history has swirled past the "guild"; some has disrupted it; some has transformed it; some has swept it entirely away. Much of the Renaissance occurred completely outside the university. The university was generally allied against the Reformation, although bitter fights were fought within many universities, and in some the reformers emerged triumphant. The industrial, democratic, and scientific revolutions have gradually moved in on the universities and changed them almost beyond recognition. Some revolutions, like the French and Russian, placed the "guild" fully under state control, although it has regained some of its ancient rights in France. In all of these intellectual and social revolutions, the university, as an institution, was initially more a "stronghold of reaction" than a revolutionary force, although the ideas of its individual members have often been a stimulus to change.

Eric Ashby has said that policy should "seep gradually upward" within the guild.[17] Sometimes it has. In Oxford and Cambridge, research of extraordinary quality developed when the guild was still in control and still devoted to the classics. But, generally, change, when it has come, has been initiated or at least assisted from outside the gates, as the case of England today so decisively demonstrates. The educational revolution now going on there comes from the outside and above, and finds its greatest proponents in the Labour Party.

The individual faculty member, and particularly the political liberal on the faculty, is often torn between the "guild" and the "socialist" views of the university. The guild view stands for self-determination, and for resistance against the administration and the trustees; the socialist view, for service to society which the administration and the trustees often represent. The guild view is elitist toward the external environment, conservative toward internal change, conformist in relation to the opinion of colleagues. The socialist view is democratic toward society, radical toward change, and nonconformist. And the political liberal is drawn toward both views. Here is a paradox. Few institutions are so conservative as the universities about their own affairs while their members are so liberal about the affairs of others; and sometimes the most liberal faculty member in one context is the most conservative in another. The natural radical, within the context of the guild, is radically conservative. The faculty member who gets arrested as a "freedom rider" in the South is a flaming supporter of unanimous prior faculty consent to any change whatsoever on his campus in the North. The door to the faculty club leads both out and in.

Change is a traumatic experience for an academic community, as for others. The Yale faculty in 1828 rejected in theory, while proving in practice, that colleges "by being immovably moored to the same station . . . serve only to measure the rapid current of improvement which is passing by them."[18] In a very real sense, the faculty is the university—its most productive element, its source of distinction. And faculty members are properly partners in the enterprise with areas reserved for their exclusive control. Yet when change comes it is rarely at the instigation of this group of partners as a collective body. The group is more likely to accept or reject or comment, than to devise and propose. The group serves a purpose as a balance wheel—resisting some things that should be resisted, insisting on more thorough discussion of some things that should be more thoroughly discussed, delaying some developments where delay gives time to adjust more gracefully to the inevitable. All this yields a greater sense of order and stability.

Institutional changes are coming, however, in areas under faculty control or influence. Some of the needed revisions will be troublesome. In many places, curricula and calendars will need to be restudied; undergraduate teaching renovated; faculty concepts of equality of treatment revised; mechanization of some elements of instruction installed; some fields of study (like biol-

ogy) revolutionized. These changes will come in the face of much
faculty hesitation and even some resistance. At least two changes,
however, will have faculty support. One will be directed toward
overcoming the fractionalization of the intellectual world, and
the other will call for procedures devised to make administration
more personal, including faculty administration.

The faculty world seems to sense a loss of unity—intellectual
and communal unity. In large measure this can be attributed to
"the overwhelming predominance of things that are new over
things that are old" and to what Robert Oppenheimer calls "a
thinning of common knowledge."[19] Knowledge is now in so
many bits and pieces and administration so distant that faculty
members are increasingly figures in a "lonely crowd," intellectu-
ally and institutionally. It is a sad commentary on the "community of masters" when its elements come together in interchange
only when they coalesce feverishly over a grievance about some
episode related to a change of the calendar or a parking fee.

Quite fortunately, however, there is a kind of senatorial courtesy within the collective faculty about changes desired by a
single member, or a few. Changes initiated from the outside, as
in the development of the federal grant university, which also
have their internal supporters, are especially easy to accomplish.
The individual faculty member seeking something new has, in
turn, often found his greatest encouragement and leverage coming from the outside; the individual scholar is the inventor, the
outside agency the force for innovation. The inventing faculty
member almost instinctively knows that internal change will
come more easily if he obtains the external support of a foundation or a federal agency. These outside-to-inside and inside-to-
outside alliances have been great sources of progress.

Much change also takes place largely outside collective faculty
purview, outside the "veto groups" of the academic commu-

nity—in the new department or institute, the new project, the new campus. The institute, in particular, has been as much the vehicle of innovation in recent years as the department has been the vault of tradition. Change comes more through spawning the new than reforming the old.

When change does come, it may be by the slow process of persuasion, or by subversion as through the inside-outside alliance, or by evasion as in the new enterprise, or by external decision. The academic community, regardless of the particular process involved, is more changed than changing; change is more unplanned than planned.

"Remembrance of things past." If the collective faculties represent the present, the collective alumni represent the past—as much the best of the past as the faculty the best of the present. The alumni are oriented toward their own undergraduate days. There seems to be a rising sense of alumni concern as the rate of change rises. Generally it is over the preservation of an emphasis on teaching as against research; of the beauty of the old campus as against the asphalt and concrete and glass of the recent "improvements"; of the quality of remembered undergraduate life in its totality; of the old admission requirements which let the old grads get in; of athletic teams that never lost a game; of the spirit of the "halls of ivy" as against the technological materialism of the federal grant university; of the integrity of the old alma mater against the blandishments from Washington. The older and the smaller and the more private and the more distinguished the university, the greater the intensity of these concerns.

If the alumni are concerned, the undergraduate students are restless. Recent changes in the American university have done them little good—lower teaching loads for the faculty, larger classes, the use of substitute teachers for the regular faculty, the choice of faculty members based on research accomplishments rather than instructional capacity, the fragmentation of knowledge into endless subdivisions. There is an incipient revolt of undergraduate students against the faculty; the revolt that used to be against the faculty *in loco parentis* is now against the faculty *in absentia*. The students find themselves under a blanket of impersonal rules for admissions, for scholarships, for examinations, for degrees. It is interesting to watch how a faculty intent on few rules for itself can fashion such a plethora of them for the students. The students also want to be treated as distinct individuals.

If the faculty looks on itself as a guild, the undergraduate students are coming to look upon themselves more as a "class"; some may even feel like a "lumpen proletariat." Lack of faculty concern for teaching, endless rules and requirements, and impersonality are the inciting causes. A few of the "nonconformists" have another kind of revolt in mind. They seek, instead, to turn the university, on the Latin American or Japanese models, into a fortress from which they can sally forth with impunity to make their attacks on society.

If federal grants for research brought a major revolution, then the resultant student sense of neglect may bring a minor counterrevolt, although the target of the revolt is a most elusive one.

The big state universities are most vulnerable to charges of neglect of students. The private universities, tied more to tradition, to student tuition, to alumni support, to smaller size, have generally far better preserved their devotion to undergraduate life.

In inter-university competition, the distribution of the ablest students, as shown by the statistics on scholarship winners, is a telling point. A university's share of the ablest students is an important element in its ranking: how attractive is its educational program to the students most entitled to make a choice?

Student pressures for better undergraduate instruction may be supplemented by the complaints of parents, who think their children are being sacrificed on the altar of research. Also, the public at large, whose attention has been riveted on the elementary and secondary schools as the "population bulge" has affected them, may now turn its attention increasingly to the university level when the "bulge" reaches there. Generally the public is more interested in quality of instruction than in quantity of research. The spotlight which the universities have helped turn on the teaching of others at lower levels may now be turned on their own.

External imperatives.   The truly major changes in university life have been initiated from the outside, by such forces as Napoleon in France, ministers of education in Germany, royal commissions and the University Grants Committee in Great Britain, the Communist Party in Russia, the emperor at the time of the Restoration in Japan, the lay university governing boards and the federal Congress in the United States—and also, in the United States, by the foundations. The foundations, quickly responsive to needs and possibilities, have been the main instruments, for example, in the reform of medical education, the introduction of interdisciplinary studies, the involvement of universities in world affairs. As catalysts, their influence has been enormous. The new developments might have been undertaken within the universities themselves, but they were not.

Prospective changes can be identified, in part, by the interests of the external initiators—trustees, state governments, foundations, industry, the federal government. What are the current concerns? There are:

problems related to costs, identified particularly by Beardsley Ruml—faculty-student ratios, fuller utilization of the calendar, excessive numbers of courses, mechanization of instruction;[20]

problems related to accommodation of the vast numbers of young people already knocking on the doors;

problems related to public service—cultural programs, urban extension, advice to state and federal legislators and agencies;

problems related to the supply of trained personnel for industry and the public, particularly engineers, scientists, and doctors;

questions about the quality and availability of research, particularly the establishment of additional university research centers;

problems related to the exploitation of new discoveries, particularly in the biological sciences and spreading out into the health sciences and agriculture.

Additionally there is a general public concern with "morality" on the campus; with the so-called beatniks, with the young radicals, with cheating, and with sex. There is also a deep concern about how far, and how fast, research discoveries may change the lives of everyone. These "moral" concerns fill the incoming mailbox of the administrator.

The external origin of most changes raises very grave problems: how to identify the "good" and the "bad," and how to embrace the good and resist the bad. There is also a problem of timing—how to adjust not too rapidly and not too slowly. And there are the problems of how to change the content of the university without changing its essential forms; of how to reconcile the conservatism of the collective faculty with the radical function of the total institution as carried out primarily by the individual faculty members. These obligations to select the good and reject the bad, to pace the rate of change, and to discover the methods of change that will do least damage to traditional processes fall primarily on the reluctant shoulders of the administrator. And as Cornford remarked: "You think (do you not?) that you have only to state a reasonable case, and people must listen to reason and act upon it at once. It is just this conviction that makes you so unpleasant."[21]

Today, changes are occurring quite rapidly and spontaneously. In addition, inter-university rivalry has become so intense that the rate of acceptance of change has been accelerated. The current problem is not so much that the university does not fully control the direction of its own development—it seldom has—but rather that it must make what are judged to be essential adjustments so often and so quickly, like an amoeba in an unfriendly environment. This has added to the strains placed on the internal structure of the institution. At the same time, however, the current rate of growth in numbers helps to relieve these strains, for a period of growth necessarily involves considerable flexibility. Still, the major test of the modern American university is how wisely and how quickly it adjusts to the important new possibilities. The great universities of the future will be those which have adjusted rapidly and effectively.

The New Faces of Change

The universities are currently facing three great areas of related adjustments: growth, shifting academic emphases, and involvement in the life of society. The direction of adjustment in each of these areas is reasonably clear; the detailed arrangements and the timing are not.

1. *Growth.* The number of university and college students in the United States will almost double during the 1960's. This addition of three million will duplicate in one decade the growth of the three centuries since Harvard was founded. The proportion of graduate students will rise considerably, and there are already 25,000 postdoctoral students.

Existing campuses are being enlarged and many new ones founded. This will be the greatest period of campus renovation and establishment in American history. A particularly large number of junior colleges will be formed as the junior college movement becomes nationwide.

New centers of graduate strength are emerging, and a network of alliances is being formed among the old and the new centers in the competition to offer the greatest total combination of resources.

To accommodate the great increase in enrollments, many calendars are being rearranged, particularly in state-supported institutions, to permit more nearly year-round use of physical facilities. Students will be able to accelerate their work if they wish, and generally students will come and go with less reference to their "class"; more of them will drop in and drop out as suits their particular schedules and needs.

There will be some further mechanization of instruction (television, language laboratories, programmed learning) to improve quality and to save faculty time for other endeavors, including more individual work with students. The sciences will almost eagerly embrace these aids to learning. The foreign language departments will be rather reluctant, because these devices can threaten their structure of faculty employment and the recruitment and utilization of graduate students.

Because of the competition for faculty members, salaries will continue to rise; fringe benefits of all sorts will be devised to tie professors to a particular campus. In addition to competition among universities, there is also intensified competition with industry and government. This competition has obvious advantages in raising faculty income but it has its negative aspects. As the market becomes more active, internal equity will be injured, for some disciplines are much more in demand in the market than others. Teaching loads will be competitively reduced, some-times to zero, although more teachers are needed and students are complaining about lack of attention. The identification of the professor with his university will be generally loosened—he will become more a member of a free-floating profession. The rules regarding how much time a professor can spend away from his university assignments and those affecting the sources of his income within the university will continue to be in great flux.

This current phenomenon of rising salaries and benefits, how-ever, may be of relatively short duration, lasting, perhaps, for the remainder of this decade. Faculty salaries have been catching up with incomes in other professions after an historical lag. By 1970, also, the personnel deficit of today may be turning into the surplus of tomorrow as all the new Ph.D.'s roll into the market. A new plateau of compensation may be reached in the 1970's. But in the long run, it is common labor more than uncommon talent that is rising in its comparative monetary evaluation, as the educational process uncovers more talent and depletes the ranks of those willing to do common labor.

2. *Shifting academic emphases.* Knowledge is exploding along with population. There is also an explosion in the need for certain skills. The university is responding to all these explosions.

The vastly increased needs for engineers, scientists, and doc-tors will draw great resources to these areas of the university. Also, some new professions are being born. Others are becoming more formally professional, for example, business administra-tion and social work. The university becomes the chief port of entry for these professions. In fact, a profession gains its identity by *making* the university the port of entry. This creates new roles for education; but it is also part of the process of freezing the structure of the occupational pyramid and assuring that the well-behaved do advance, even if the geniuses do not. The university is used as an egg-candling device; and it is, perhaps, a better one than any other that can be devised, but the process takes some of the adventure out of occupational survival, and does for some professions what the closed shop has done for some unions. The life of the universities for a thousand years has been tied into the recognized professions in the surrounding society, and the universities will continue to respond as new professions arise.

The fastest-growing intellectual field today is biology. Here there is a veritable revolution where the doctrine of evolution once reigned supreme. To the classifying efforts of the past are being added the new analytical methods of the present, often drawn from chemistry and physics. There are levels of complexity to be explored in all living structures. The "code of life" can now be read; soon it will be understood, and soon after that, used. It is an intellectual discovery of unique and staggering proportions. The secrets of the atom, much as they have changed and are changing human activity on this planet, may hold no greater significance than the secrets still hidden in the genetic code. If the first half of the twentieth century may be said to have belonged to the physical sciences, the second half may well belong to the biological. Resources within the universities will be poured into the new biology and into the resulting new medicine and agriculture, well supported though medicine and agriculture already are.

Another field ready to bloom is that of the creative arts, hitherto the ugly ducklings or Cinderellas of the academic world. America is bursting with creativity in painting, music, literature, the theater with a vigor equaled in few other parts of the world today. Italy, France, Spain, Germany, Russia, England, the Low Countries have had great periods of cultural flowering. America is having one now. In the arts the universities have been more hospitable to the historian and the critic than to the creator; he has found his havens elsewhere. Yet it is the creativity of science that has given science its prestige in the university. Perhaps creativity will do the same again for the humanities, though there may be less new to create than has recently been true in science and the tests of value are far less precise. A very important role remains for the historian of past ages of creativity and for the critic of the current productions. But the universities need to find ways also to accommodate pure creative effort if they are to have places on stage as well as in the wings and in the audience in the great drama of cultural growth now playing on the American stage.

These possibilities for expansion—in the training of engineers, scientists, doctors, and the newer professionals, in biology, and in the creative arts, among various others—raise again the problem of balance. As James Bryant Conant has noted, the Western world has had for a thousand years a continuing problem of "keeping a balance between the advancement of knowledge, professional education, general education, and the demands of student life."[22]

But the balance is always changing; this is the unbalancing reality. The balance is not equal treatment, the provision of equal time in some mechanical and eternal way between teaching and research, or between the humanities and science. The dynamics of balance did not give equal treatment to the available scientist in Padua in 1300 when Giotto was painting his chapel, or to the available artist in Padua in 1600 when Galileo was lecturing from his crude platform. Balance cannot be determined on the scales by blind justice, field versus field and activity versus activity.

The essence of balance is to match support with the intellectual creativity of subject fields; with the need for skills of the highest level; with the kinds of expert service that society currently most requires. None of these measures is constant. Balance requires, therefore, a shifting set of judgments which relates facilities and attention to the possibilities inherent in each field, each skill, each activity at that moment of time in that environment, yet preserves for all fields their essential integrity. To know balance is to know the potential creativity, the potential productivity, the potential contribution of each competing activity in an unfolding pattern of time and an evolving landscape of environment. To know balance is to know more than anyone can ever know in advance. But decisions must nevertheless be made and time will tell how well. The only certainly wrong decision is that the balance of today must be preserved for tomorrow. Where will the world's work and the university's work best be done? The answer to that question is the true definition of balance.

3. *Involvement in the life of society.* Knowledge is now central to society. It is wanted, even demanded, by more people and more institutions than ever before. The university as producer, wholesaler and retailer of knowledge cannot escape service. Knowledge, today, is for everybody's sake.

The campus and society are undergoing a somewhat reluctant and cautious merger, already well advanced. M.I.T. is at least as much related to industry and government as Iowa State ever was to agriculture. Extension work is really becoming "life-long learning." Harvard today has four post-graduate doctors in its medical school for every one still working for his degree; so also for many other skills including business. Television makes it possible for extension to reach into literally every home; the boundaries of the university are stretched to embrace all of society. The student becomes alumnus and the alumnus continues as student; the graduate enters the outside world and the public enters the classroom and the laboratory. Knowledge has the terrifying potential of becoming popular, opening a Pandora's box.

The campus becomes a center for cultural life; it has a ready-made audience in its students and faculty and it has the physical facilities. Persons attracted by the performing and visual arts and the lectures come to live around the campus—also assorted crackpots. As the downtown area in some cities decays, the campus takes its place as the cultural center of the community. A new dimension has been added to the land grant idea of service.

The New Deal took professors to Washington from many campuses, the New Frontier from more than just one. In Wisconsin before World War I, the campus and the state house in Madison were exceptionally close. Today the campus is being drawn to the city hall and the state capital as never before. The politicians need new ideas to meet the new problems; the agencies need expert advice on how to handle the old. The professor can supply both. Keynes concluded his *General Theory* as follows: ". . . the ideas of economists and political philosophers, both when they are right and when they are wrong, are more powerful than is commonly understood. Indeed the world is ruled by little else. Practical men, who believe themselves to be quite exempt from any intellectual influences, are usually the slaves of some defunct economist. Madmen in authority, who hear voices in the air, are distilling their frenzy from some academic scribbler of a few years back. I am sure that the power of vested interests is vastly exaggerated compared with the gradual encroachment of ideas."[23] As, for example, the ideas of Keynes.

The university must range itself on the side of intelligent solutions to sometimes unintelligent questions. These questions more and more arise from abroad as well as at home; and the quality of the answers has been made all the more crucial in a world swept by Communist and nationalist revolutions.

There are those who fear the further involvement of the university in the life of society. They fear that the university will lose its objectivity and its freedom. But society is more desirous of objectivity and more tolerant of freedom than it used to be. The university can be further ahead of the times and further behind the times, further to the left of the public and further to the right of the public—and still keep its equilibrium—than was ever the case before, although problems in this regard are not yet entirely unknown. There are those who fear that the university will be drawn too far from basic to applied research and from applied research to application itself. But the lines dividing these never have been entirely clear and much new knowledge has been generated at the borders of basic and applied research, and even of applied knowledge and its application.

Growth and shifting emphases and involvement in society all take money; and which universities get it in the largest quantities will help determine which of them excel a decade or two hence. Will federal support be spent according to merit or according to political power? Will private donors continue to do as well as they recently have for those universities that have done well already? Will the states find new sources of revenue or will their expenditures be held under a lid of no new taxes? The answers to these questions will help predict the standings on the next rating scale of universities.

However this turns out, the scene of American higher education will continue to be marked by great variety, and this is one of its great strengths. The large and the small, the private and the public, the general and the specialized all add their share to over-all excellence. The total system is extraordinarily flexible, decentralized, competitive—and productive. The new can be tried, the old tested with considerable skill and alacrity. Pluralism in higher education matches the pluralistic American society. The multiversity, in particular, is the child of middle-class pluralism; it relates to so much of the variety of the surrounding society and is thus so varied internally.

The general test of higher education is not how much is done poorly, and some is; rather it is how much is done superbly, and a great deal is, to the nation's great benefit. Although it has been said that the best universities in America have been caught in a "stalemate of success,"[24] there is no stalemate; there is some success.

Changes Still To Come

There has been some success, but there are some problems still to be fully faced; and they are problems of consequence.

One is the improvement of undergraduate instruction in the university. It will require the solution of many sub-problems: how to give adequate recognition to the teaching skill as well as to the research performance of the faculty; how to create a curriculum that serves the needs of the student as well as the research interests of the teacher; how to prepare the generalist as well as the specialist in an age of specialization looking for better generalizations; how to treat the individual student as a unique human being in the mass student body; how to make the university seem smaller even as it grows larger; how to establish a range of contact between faculty and students broader than the one-way route across the lectern or through the television screen; how to raise educational policy again to the forefront of faculty concerns. Increasingly, also, the better institutions will need to keep in mind that many of their undergraduate students will be going on to graduate school, and therefore that they need individual attention as pre-graduate students.

Another major task is to create a more unified intellectual world. We need to make contact between the two, the three, the many cultures; to open channels of intelligent conversation across the disciplines and divisions; to close the gap between C. P. Snow's

"Luddites" and scientists;[25] to answer fragmentation with general theories and sensitivities. Even philosophy, which once was the hub of the intellectual universe, is now itself fragmented into such diverse specialties as mathematics and semantics. However, the physical sciences are drawing together as new discoveries create more basic general theories; the biological sciences may be pulled together in the process now going on; the social sciences might be unified around the study of organizations and the relations of individuals to and within them. Chemistry and social psychology may come to be central focalizing fields. As knowledge is drawn together, if in fact it is, a faculty may again become a community of masters; but "a sense of the unity . . . of all knowledge"[26] is still a very long way off.

A third problem is to relate administration more directly to individual faculty and students in the massive institution. We need to decentralize below the campus level to the operating agencies; to make the collective faculty a more vital, dynamic, progressive force as it now is only at the departmental level; to bridge the growing chasm between the department that does the teaching and the institute that does the research, with the faculty member torn between; to make the old departments and divisions more compatible with the new divisions of knowledge; to make it possible for an institution to see itself in totality rather than just piecemeal and in the sweep of history rather than just at a moment of time; to bring an understanding of both internal and external realities to all those intimately related to the process, so that there may be greater understanding; to see to it that administration serves and stimulates rather than rules the institution, that it be expendable when necessary and flexible all the time; to assure that the university can do better what it does best; to solve the whole range of governmental problems within the university.

Additionally, there is the urgent issue of how to preserve a margin for excellence in a populist society, when more and more of the money is being spent on behalf of all of the people. The great university is of necessity elitist—the elite of merit—but it operates in an environment dedicated to an egalitarian philosophy. How may the contribution of the elite be made clear to the egalitarians, and how may an aristocracy of intellect justify itself to a democracy of all men? It was equality of opportunity, not equality *per se,* that animated the founding fathers and the progress of the American system; but the forces of populist equality have never been silent, the battle between Jeffersonianism and Jacksonianism never finally settled.

If there are to be new departures, they are most likely to come on the campuses of those old, private universities which have prided themselves on control of their own destiny, and on the totally new campuses of the state universities in America and the new public universities in Britain. The university for the twenty-first century is more likely to emerge from these environments than from any others. Out of the pride of the old and the vacuum of the new may come the means to make undergraduate life more exciting, intellectual discourse more meaningful, administration more human. And perhaps there will arise a more dynamic demonstration of how excellence makes democracy more vital and its survival more assured. Then the universities may rise to "the heights of the times" and overcome "their inspirational poverty."[27]

George Beadle, president of the University of Chicago, once implied that the very large American university (but not his own) might be like the dinosaur which "became extinct because he grew larger and larger and then sacrificed the evolutionary flexibility he needed to meet changing conditions";[28] its body became too large for its brain. David Riesman has spoken of the leading

American universities as "directionless . . . as far as major innovations are concerned";[29] they have run out of foreign models to imitate; they have lost their "ferment." The fact is that they are not directionless; they have been moving in clear directions and with considerable speed; there has been no "stalemate." But these directions have not been set as much by the university's visions of its destiny as by the external environment, including the federal government, the foundations, the surrounding and sometimes engulfing industry.

The university has been embraced and led down the garden path by its environmental suitors; it has been so attractive and so accommodating; who could resist it and why would it, in turn, want to resist?

But the really new problems of today and tomorrow may lend themselves less to solutions by external authority; they may be inherently problems for internal resolution. The university may now again need to find out whether it has a brain as well as a body.

The Cities of Intellect

We have been speaking of the City of Intellect as a university city with its satellite suburbs. The City of Intellect may be viewed in a broader context, encompassing all the intellectual resources of a society, and the even broader perspective of the force of intellect as the central force of a society—its soul. Will it be the salvation of our society?

The organized intellect is a great machine that has gained extraordinary momentum since the Greeks got it going 2500 years ago. It turns out its countless new pieces of knowledge but with little thought for their consequences—their impact on the environment—like a new insecticide. Its attention to problems quite naturally does not always relate primarily to their importance but often, instead, to the possibility of their solution. Thus the problems of rising population and rising levels of destructive capacity move along without study commensurate with their inherent significance. Does this machine have within it the "seeds of its own destruction"? Or can it develop an over-all rationality? As Lee DuBridge of Cal Tech has said: "Scientists and engineers do worry about the consequences of their works. But neither they nor anyone else has discovered how to avoid or even to predict these consequences."[30]

The process cannot be stopped. The results cannot be foreseen. It remains to adapt. And here the social sciences and humanities may find their particular roles in helping to define the good as well as the true and to add wisdom to truth. It may not be the conflict of cultures that is so crucial but rather the rate at which each culture moves forward. Can the intellect come to handle all the problems it creates in the course of solving other problems? Can the university help solve the growing war between the future and the past? Can the span of intellectual comprehension be widened spatially and temporally?

Intellect has also become an instrument of national purpose, a component part of the "military-industrial complex." Our Western City of Intellect finds its counterpart or counterparts in the East. In the war of the ideological worlds, a great deal depends on the use of this instrument. Knowledge is durable. It is also transferable. Knowledge costs a great deal to produce, less to reproduce. Thus it only pays to produce knowledge if through production it can be put into use better and faster. The Communist City of Intellect has been a planned community. It grows only in certain directions and in certain ways. This allows concentration of effort but limits growth and recognition except in restricted segments of the intellectual world. This City flourishes in science and in military might but lags in the humanities and the social sciences. Whole areas that would be covered by a really modern City of Intellect are largely unpopulated.

The two Cities of Intellect are not only sources of weapons— they also form a potential bridge between their two societies. Knowledge is universal. Its creators generally prefer freedom. To the extent the Eastern City of Intellect grows and makes contact with the Western, it almost inevitably changes its own society. Here a certain type of society really may carry the "seeds of its own destruction." It either competes and changes, or it loses some of its over-all power of competition.

Marx saw technology as the major force in history; but intellect creates technology and the logic of intellect's development may be quite different from the unraveling of the "mode of production" as Marx visualized it. History has seldom, if ever, proved a theorist to be so incorrect and at the same time so influential as Marx. The wave of the future may more nearly be middle-class democracy,[31] with all its freedoms, through its better use of intellect in all intellect's many dimensions, than the "dictatorship of the proletariat" (which, in fact, is the dictatorship of the single party). But it has not yet been proved conclusively whether intellect can preserve and even create the culture of freedom, in which it best flourishes, more effectively than technology, under Communist leadership, can be used to bolster dictatorship.

The intellect, and the university as its most happy home, can have great potential roles to play in the reconciliation of the war between the future and the past, and the solution—one way or the other—of the war between the ideological giants who now rend the world with their struggles. Certain it is, however, that the reconciliation of the future and the past can only be made more elusive in the context of an ideological struggle where survival is almost the sole essence of rational behavior. The two problems compound each other's effects.

At the outset I quoted Cardinal Newman on his "Idea of a University," reflecting the beautiful ivory tower of Oxford as it once was. It seems appropriate to conclude with Alfred North Whitehead's prophetic words in 1916 on the place of intellect: "In the conditions of modern life, the rule is absolute: the race which does not value trained intelligence is doomed. Not all your heroism, not all your social charm, not all your wit, not all your victories on land or sea, can move back the finger of fate. Today we maintain ourselves. Tomorrow science will have moved forward yet one more step, and there will be no appeal from the judgment which will be pronounced on the uneducated."[32]

These are the uses of the university.

4

RECONSIDERATIONS
AFTER THE REVOLTS
OF THE 1960's

Much has happened to higher education and to the United States since these lectures were written in the early spring of 1963 and presented at Harvard toward the end of April of that year. That was a conservative period in higher education—not in the sense that nothing was happening, for a great deal was, but in the sense that what was happening was mostly adding quantity and quality to what was already being done. The directions then generally appeared to be quite clear to most: to accommodate the tidal wave of students and to expand and improve research capabilities, particularly in science. Yet the early signs of a new period of reform, and even of revolt and counter-revolt, were already evident, as these lectures then noted.

Cardinal Newman wrote in 1852 about the classical British university when it was already beginning to be conquered by the German model, and conquered even in Britain. Abraham Flexner portrayed in 1930 the ideal of the German research university after it had long given way to the American version of greater service orientation in the United States and as it was about to give way to the Nazi-dominated university in Germany. These Godkin lectures, in turn, described the American model just before it met its greatest challenges after a century of development and growth.

One may wonder whether a model comes into somewhat clearer sight only as it exits from the stage of history and makes way for some new institutional participant with a quite different character. Whether or not a slow exit is what is now happening to the American model, I do not think that anyone can yet be sure. Will 1870 to 1970 have been the century of the rise and the beginning of the decline of the American university? Or, after a pause for a time of troubles, will it gain new strength and rise to greater heights? I leave this simply as a question, for this chapter is concerned, not with what has happened since 1963 or what may happen in the future, but, rather, with how I now wish I had written these lectures *in 1963*. To begin with, however, I should like to reaffirm my conviction about the continuing validity of certain of the central themes.

Themes Reaffirmed

Many, and even most, of the themes of 1963 have been accented by intervening events—a few in a rather spectacular fashion:

1. The "new centrality" of the university is now even more widely recognized, not only because the university adds to knowledge and extends the uses of knowledge in an age of ever newer knowledge, but also because political and cultural changes, in part, originate within it. The university has even been said recently to be the "paramount institution" in "post-industrial society."[1]

2. The modern university was presented as a "new type of

institution"—and new largely because of the new centrality of knowledge—with "a whole series of communities" within it rather than being a "single community" as it once had been and as it was customarily still viewed. The university was seen as both more central to society and also changed within itself. As the many internal fissions have emerged in recent years, it has become increasingly apparent that the university "means many things to . . . many different people," and that neither all of these many things nor all of these different people are fully unified with each other. What was called in 1963 a "multiversity" has, in fact, on occasion, become a Tower of Babel partially falling apart rather than being held loosely together.

3. Consensus and tolerance were set forth as essential to keeping intact the "whole uneasy balance" of the multiversity. I called it an "inconsistent" institution that could survive best only as the "moderates" kept control. "Extremists" could turn the situation quickly into "war." So many possible points of conflict could be exploited.

The loss of consensus and of tolerance over the past decade has indeed led to many campus wars as the potential points of conflict, previously partially obscured by a history of unbroken peace, became actual points of conflict—students versus faculty, humanists versus scientists, younger versus older faculty members, and so forth. Below the placid surface of 1963 lurked the largely unsuspected strains. A narrow barrier of tolerance stood between peace and war—not much separated them from each other—and, when tolerance was gone, what had been unbroken peace became intermittent warfare. The "delicate balance" was delicate indeed.

4. The organized faculty was presented as having a "guild mentality" marked by resistance to change in its essential internal affairs except as a slow collegial unanimity emerged. The

university has been shocked by many external and internal crises over the past few years, but it is remarkable not how much has changed but how little has changed on so many campuses in those areas that are under faculty control and where the faculty feels strongly about its control.[2] The more the environment has changed, the more the organized faculty has remained the same. It has been the greatest single point of institutional conservatism in recent times, as it has been historically. Little that it has held dear and that it could control has been allowed to change.

5. The period of 1870 to 1920 was presented as the era of the president, when "giants" led the way in dramatic changes, and the period since 1920 as one of "administrators" instead of giants. A period of stability in goals and methods, as from 1920 to 1960, tends to be one marked by the rise of academic administrators surrounded by faculty power. The theme was that giants were most likely to emerge in a period of rapid change in goals or methods or both. We are now entering such a period once again, or so it now seems, and some new presidential giants are needed to give leadership to the changes. Virtually all successful major reforms or revolutions in the academic world have come into being and probably will continue to come into being through leadership from the top—or from the outside—through the instrumentality of an Eliot, or a Napoleon.

6. The federal influence from the outside was already being felt in 1963—the "federal grant university" had arrived. In retrospect, the two great new forces of the 1960's were the federal government and the protesting students. The federal government emphasized science and research, equality of opportunity, impartiality of treatment among the races, and the innovative role of the federal agency. Much of what has happened to the campus, both good and evil, in the past decade can be laid at the door of the federal government. For the first time in American history

there was a growing sense and an increasing reality of the presence of the federal colossus in higher education. And this reality will never go away again. The federal grant university is now on the way to having added to it the federal grant college, as federal aid and influence permeate all the institutions of higher education and not just a few selected universities alone. University and college presidents now cultivate Washington as avidly as they have cultivated state capitals and the Captains of Industry.

7. "Involvement in the life of society" has grown greatly. The campus has even been drawn to the "city hall," and the predicted "Pandora's box" may well have been opened. How to serve the city, as the rural community has long been served, is now a perplexing problem for many campuses. New pressure groups are insisting that knowledge really be for "everybody's sake." The campus still debates involvement while strong elements in society insist upon it.

8. Some of what were then seen as the "changes still to come" are now upon us, often with a vengeance. The "improvement of undergraduate instruction" is now a lively and even abrasive subject on many campuses. The need to create "a more unified intellectual world" that looks at society broadly, rather than through the eyes of the narrow specialist, has now become the insistent demand of students for relevance. The need "to solve the whole range of governmental problems within the university" is now recognized as the battle over governance. "How to preserve a margin for excellence" in an increasingly egalitarian society has become a most intense issue. It takes the form not only of the lesser versus the greater research institutions seeking funds and preferment—the state college against the university—but also, within the elite institutions, of demands by some students and faculty members for open admissions, no course requirements, no grades. The populists are inside as well as outside

the gates of the elite institutions, and the current cry for equality of result is replacing the older call for equality of opportunity. Academic reform, governance, demands for equality, in a few swift years, have moved up on the agenda from prospective new business to urgent old business.

9. The "incipient revolt" of students is now a national trauma, viewed recently by the public as the Number 1 or Number 2 social issue. In 1963, people were still talking about the apathetic generation, the graduating classes of organization men, the uncommitted students. But apathy quickly turned to activism, organization men to anti-establishmentarians, the uncommitted to the new radicals. In 1963, the possibility of such a sudden change in the academic weather was only dimly seen when seen at all. There were, however, as I then noted, already the "walking wounded" within the multiversity; some students were beginning to visualize themselves as a "lumpen proletariat"—or, in more modern terminology, as prisoners in the campus ghetto; and a few students wanted even then to make the campus into a "fortress" from which society might be attacked.

The "minor counterrevolt" of undergraduate students against their deteriorating situation that I thought likely in 1963 became, instead, a major revolt even as early as 1964; and the walking wounded were soon found among the faculty and the administrators as well as the students. That small cloud, so seldom noticed on the horizon in 1963, quickly materialized into a series of cyclones.

10. The public backlash was already gathering in 1963, even before the great frontlash of the student revolt occurred. There was even then concern with the "beatniks, with the young radicals, with cheating, and with sex." These concerns later were exploited by a California political leader who campaigned with the catchy theme of Treason, Drugs and Sex on the campus. The

public was also worried about "how far, and how fast, research discoveries may change the lives of everyone." The university was accelerating its racing car named Science, hardly noticing that the public was getting ready to reduce the supply of gas. These several public complaints were already filling the "incoming mailbox of the administrator" in 1963. The mail turned into votes and the votes turned into actions faster than had seemed possible; and more than one state got a governor who attacked higher education.

Reconsiderations

What might in 1963 have been said better or differently or, perhaps, not at all? I shall set forth four major revisions which I wish I had then been wise enough, or cautious enough, to undertake.

1. The term "multiversity" was used in an effort to make clear that we had a new phenomenon, a new kind of university. The older term of university carried with it the older visions of a unified "community of masters and students" with a single "soul" or purpose. There was, however, a new reality and it seemed that it would be helpful to have a new word to carry the image of this new reality; to make the point that Alma Mater was less an integrated and eternal spirit, and more a split and variable personality; to call attention to the fact that what had once been a community was now more like an environment—more like a city, a "city of infinite variety." Thus the word—"multiversity." It was intended as a descriptive phrase; it has, however, become, on the lips of some, a term of opprobrium.

The word was not really new with me. I later learned that it had been used in an internal faculty report at a midwestern university and by a faculty member at Cornell. It had also been employed by presidents of two of the Big Ten universities[3] and perhaps by others. The word, thus, was in the air, and had several more or less simultaneous authors.

It turned out to be a word that was easily misunderstood. A number of people thought it was "multi-university" in the sense of a multi-campus institution. The multi-campus institution is also a recent phenomenon of great importance—40 percent of all college and university students are now in multi-campus institutions—but it is quite a separate, although somewhat related, development. It should have been clear that the "multiversity" was viewed primarily as a single-campus phenomenon since modern Harvard was given as the first illustration of the multi-faceted campus.

What I meant by the word was that the modern university was a "pluralistic" institution—pluralistic in several senses: in having several purposes, not one; in having several centers of power, not one; in serving several clienteles, not one. It worshiped no single God; it constituted no single, unified community; it had no discretely defined set of customers. It was marked by many visions of the Good, the True, and the Beautiful, and by many roads to achieve these visions; by power conflicts; by service to many markets and concern for many publics. It might have been called a pluralistic university; or a conglomerate university—making an analogy to business; or, as some Germans now do, the comprehensive university; or a number of other things.[4] What I wanted to do was to mark the contrast with a more nearly single-purpose institution having a more monistic spirit, a more monolithic leadership, and a single clientele—whether the older Oxford concentrating on teaching, run by the faculty, and serving would-be gentlemen or the older Berlin concentrating on research, run by the chair professors, and serving new knowledge.

I wish I had then read William James on the "multiverse."[5] It would have given me a good footnote to employ in lectures given at Harvard and helped me to clarify my ideas. James was talking solely about philosophy. He was contrasting "pluralism" with "monism."

The monistic approach, he said, is to find a single "Absolute." Such absolutes might be (although he did not use them as illustrations) the word of God, or the class struggle of Marx, or the survival of the fittest of Darwin, or the infantile sex of Freud; some absolute that determined everything else, that lent a unity to thought, that posited a community where all the parts were internally related, where there was an organic unity with no independent parts, and that yielded an inherent consistency. James noted that such an absolute was effective in conferring mental peace, a degree of certainty.[6] The absolute (and James was against all absolutes) sought to define what was right and what was wrong in the present, to explain the past, to describe the future. It sought to provide sure standards for making decisions and a clear vision of both past and future events.

The pluralistic approach, by contrast, as James noted, sees several forces at work in more or less eternal conflict, sees everything in "flux," sees a state of indeterminism. There is said to be more free will for the individual, and more dysfunction within and between organizations. Parts of the whole, James said, "may be externally related" rather than only internally related. Thus James spoke of the "multiverse" as a situation where "each part hangs together with its very next neighbors," and where "every part" is "in some possible or mediated connexion with every other part." Thus there was a "strung-along type" of unity or a "contiguity" rather than one central absolute to which every part was tied directly. "Nothing includes everything, or dominates over everything."[7]

This may be taken also as a good description of the multiversity with its strung-along type of unity, with its lack of devotion to any single faith and its lack of concentration on any single function, with a condition of cohesion[8] at best or coexistence at next best or contiguity at least (under internal pressures in recent years, some campuses have moved from a state of cohesion to one of coexistence, or from coexistence to mere contiguity of the constituent elements). The multiversity can be compared, as James compared the multiverse, to a "federal republic" as against a "kingdom," a federal republic where attention should be paid to "each form" by itself, rather than only to "all forms" together.[9]

The multiversity, like the multiverse, has weaknesses: loyalty is not so readily given, conflicts are not so easily settled in terms of absolute principles, borders to confine the extension of efforts are harder to define. By contrast, monistic universities, based on the Bible, or the Koran, or the Communist Manifesto, or the Great Books can test loyalty more precisely, can settle disputes more on principle, can limit their functions more readily. But they also tend to be more static in a dynamic world, more intolerant in a world crying for understanding and accommodation to diversity, more closed to the unorthodox person and idea, more limited in their comprehension of total reality.

To the extent that universities are a generating force for new ideas and for critical commentary on the status quo, they are more likely to fulfill this role where Absolute confronts Absolute, where thesis meets antithesis, where one culture contests another; just as biological generation most often occurs where one ecological environment shades into another, where the sea meets the land. Should the model of the university be based more on productive conflict or on doctrinal unity, on the interaction of disparate entities or on the integration of fully compatible parts?

The multiversity is based more on conflict and on interaction; the monistic university more on unity and integration. Monistic universities are more like Plato's hierarchical Republic, and multiversities more nearly correspond to Aristotle's search for the Golden Mean. That ancient controversy, over the closed versus the open society, over rigidity of purpose and hierarchy as against constant adaptation and adjustment, has been going on for a long time in many guises, and so will the controversy between the bitter principled enemies and the reluctant pragmatic supporters of the multiversity.

The multiversity is not one thing but many things along a continuum. J. Douglas Brown sought to establish as a separate type the idea of the "liberal university,"[10] like Princeton, with its greater emphasis on teaching and on the student as a "whole man" and its lesser emphasis on professional schools and public service, with its sense of community through reliance on small size and local residence. I see the differences between Princeton and Harvard, rather, as one of degree—with Princeton toward one end of the continuum and Harvard toward the other with a highly desirable diversity in between.

To help coin a word is not the same thing as creating the institution to which it refers, although some seem to confuse the two processes. The multiversity began when professional schools were originally established, beginning with the medical school at the University of Pennsylvania in 1765; when Harvard created the first departments in 1825 and Jefferson the first separate faculties at Virginia in 1824, as against the earlier single faculty with a single curriculum; when the Morrill Land Grant Act was passed in 1862; when Eliot introduced electives in the 1870's and 1880's; when Harper started an extension service at Chicago in 1892; when the "Wisconsin Idea" was born in the early 1900's; and at many other times and in many other places when and where knowledge was subdivided, new services were added, size accumulated. William Rainey Harper's University of Chicago was being called "Harper's Bazaar" already in the 1890's.

If any group can be said to have sponsored the growth of the multiversity, it has been the faculty—choosing ever narrower specializations, emphasizing research, giving service for love and for money and for both. The spirit of the multiversity sprang particularly from the minds and the hearts of faculty members. Yet some faculty members who avidly seek to live in the multiversity, as their chosen habitat, also love to criticize it unmercifully; it is both their self-selected home and their scorned "inter-section of freeways."[11] Their actions in seeking this habitat, however, belie their words in so severely condemning it.[12] They come to this seemingly contradictory position from both the Left and the Right.

2. I wish I had not used the word "mediator" in describing one of the roles of the president or that I had explained it better—not that it is not a good word but rather that it was so generally misunderstood. "Mediator" to many people apparently means a person who merely carries messages back and forth between the parties, plays no independent leadership role, has no ideas or principles of his own. I had tried to set forth the differences in mediation approaches between seeking a current "compromise" and finding a solution that is "effective" in the long-run, and I clearly preferred the latter. But the word "mediator" to many meant unprincipled compromise, nevertheless.

I do not retract the idea that the president almost universally is, in part, a mediator of whichever type. He is and of necessity must be. His performance of this role is inherent in the nature of the multiversity. Leadership of any complex organization or society that permits considerable freedom of opinion and expression to its constituent members and groups involves mediation among the diverse elements. There are mediated connexions between "strung-along elements," as James noted, and the president is the chief mediator of these connexions.[13] More than anyone else he must interpret one group to another, set limits to conflict, referee disputes, work out acceptable solutions. This is a highly important and immensely difficult task. It is one of the highest functions of leadership.

But I wish I had used a different word with different public connotations: political leader, or community leader, or campus statesman, or unifier or peacekeeper, or chief persuader, or crisis manager or agent of integration—anything but mediator. The tone should have been conveyed of active leadership, of statesmanlike solutions, of holding the campus together against internal and external attacks, of keeping the peace as against disruption, of using ideas and principles to bind the ties, of relying on persuasion rather than on force, of seeking consent rather than governing by fiat, of being the guardian of reason in debate, decency in human relations and sanity in action, of meshing together the discordant elements into a productive entity. I wish I had made greater use of a phrase I actually did use as an alternative—the "clerk of the meeting" who both draws forth and contributes to "the sense of the meeting" in the Society of Friends.

The reaction to the word mediator startled me, partly because I have a high regard for effective mediators, as the leaders at Yale and at Ann Arbor and at Berkeley the past few years have been—people who can work out solutions to highly charged and infinitely complex situations, who can keep the place open and progressing when so many others want to shut it down. Someone must seek concessions among the many conflicting points of view on a complex campus, must find the workable compromises; otherwise the campus is abandoned to irreconcilable nonnegotiable demands on the one side and static resistance on the other; otherwise initiative is left in the hands of the fanatic reformers and the fanatic supporters of the status quo—the proponents at both extremes of no compromise.

But I was also startled at the reaction to the single word "mediator" because I talked about the "mediator-initiator" and stressed the role of the president as initiator of progress, and said that "progress is more important than peace to a university." I also spoke of the president in his role as "gladiator" fighting for "freedom and quality." But among these three roles of leadership—mediator, initiator, gladiator—the one that was remembered most was the first and with a definition of compromiser.

I said that "progress is more important than peace." I should also have pointed out that the right kind of progress in the shorter run contributes to peace in the longer run even though that progress may disturb the peace in the shorter run by arousing controversy.

I should have added a fourth presidential role. This is the role of image maker—creating a favorable image of the institution and of himself as the public symbol of the institution. In modern society, with the mass replacement of face-to-face relations by intermediate images, images become crucial. This is particularly true of a large institution with its far-flung publics. Thus the president must be concerned with his own image and the image of his institution (and the two are closely related) for the sake of the continuity and improvement of the institution. An additional reason why the president must now be concerned with his role as image maker is that his critics among the radical students and professors have been so phenomenally successful with their own image making through their dress, their rhetoric, their hair styles, and have projected themselves so spectacularly through TV and newspaper headlines; so also have some political leaders on the reactionary right been successful with their exaggerations and their simplistic slogans. Thus the fighting beret of one president was an image maker's answer to the raised fists of his image-making opponents. To fight one image it takes another more effective one, but not necessarily a beret.

But there are dangers in this role, as in each of the other three. The pursuit of image may lead to an undue concern with public credit as against private results—with how things look instead of with how things are, with what shows in the short-run as against what counts in the long-run, with a policy of selective cowardice by the president in saving himself instead of his institution. Each role has its dangers and each role confronts the other: the demands of peace can stand in the way of accepting the strains of progress, an interest in uninterrupted progress can inhibit the undertaking of costly battles for freedom and quality in the short term, and gladiatorial efforts against the external and internal opposition can ruin a carefully built image of universal acceptance and approbation. It is a difficult series of roles to fill simultaneously. And many presidents much of the time do actually choose to be "mostly a mediator".[14]

3. For the sake of some readers I should have put in bold type the phrase in the 1963 Preface that "analysis should not be confused with approval or description with defense." I was mainly concerned with analysis and description, and not with approval and defense.

There were notes of approval, however. I did refer to the "generally optimistic tone" of the approach and made reference to how "consistently productive" the multiversity was "in the search for new knowledge" and "in serving so many of the segments of an advancing civilization."

A larger number of references were made, nevertheless, to "problems" and to "changes"; and there were some critical comments: on how the university had been "led down the garden path by its environmental suitors" and how it needed "to find out whether it has a brain as well as a body." This was saying, in what I thought was blunt language, that the university better find out which profession it really was following.

Yet some people have taken analysis to be approval and description to be defense, and to assume or to claim that every act of every multiversity was both approved and defended in these lectures. Thus I learned how easily some persons who call themselves scholars can turn a descriptive "is" into a prescriptive "should be" and then attack the false "should be."

It was curious how fast the approach sometimes changed from first endorsing my criticisms of the multiversity to then claiming that I had created it on behalf of the military-industrial complex and that it should be brought to a grinding halt. At Berkeley, for example, SLATE—the predecessor group to FSM—in the *Slate Supplement* distributed in September 1964, said "we emphatically agree" with the criticisms made in *The Uses of the University* of the neglectful treatment of undergraduate students; my criticisms were taken as solid proof of the contentions advanced by SLATE. Yet some of these same students were shortly even more emphatically claiming that they disagreed with the book on the grounds that it was a defense of all aspects of the nefarious multiversity. The transition from being quoted as a respected critic to being charged as a kept-apologist was quite abrupt. The same persons leapt from one position to the other as it suited their purposes; and not just students did this. Attitudes changed quickly from agreement to condemnation as external factors intervened.

I discovered too how dangerous it can be to describe as clearly and frankly as one could the inherent nature of a controversial institution. Although description is not defense, it can be dangerous nevertheless. Some people live most happily with their cherished illusions and their comfortable myths, and recoil when the mirror of reality is held before them.[15] In particular, the professor who pictures himself as a radical for all seasons dislikes public mention of his very real conservatism about the affairs of his own faculty. One reaction is to smash the mirror.

Would more precautions have reduced the chance of distortions? I quoted Abraham Flexner's view that universities had become "service stations," and I indicated that he did not approve of "service" activities. This was turned by some into my saying that the university was a "service station" and that I did approve. I quoted Fritz Machlup of Princeton on the existence of a "knowledge industry." This phrase was then credited to me, then "industry" was turned into "factory," then the word "knowledge" was dropped, and what started out as Machlup's factual description of the "knowledge industry" became my asserted goal to turn the university into a "factory." These misuses of quotations from Flexner and Machlup are two of the cruder distortions. But this can be expected when some of the commentators are giving political reviews rather than academic reviews, like political trials versus legal trials.[16]

4. I wish that I had written the fourth chapter that I had originally intended. Heavy duties as a university president made this difficult and service on an advisory board appointed that spring by President Kennedy in connection with a major national railroad dispute made it impossible.

That chapter was to treat academic reform in general and more particularly the reforms undertaken on the new campuses of the University of California which were shortly to open—San Diego in 1964, and Irvine and Santa Cruz in 1965.[17] Two of these campuses were being organized on a cluster college basis (San Diego and Santa Cruz), one was planning to try out pass-fail grading (Santa Cruz), another was planning to experiment with having no required courses and allowing each student to choose his own programs (Irvine), one was hoping to bridge the Two Worlds of C. P. Snow (San Diego), one was looking for new ways of associating knowledge instead of parceling it out in accordance with the standard disciplinary departments (Irvine); and there were other new departures.

These at the time were the three most experimental university campuses in the United States. Planning on each of them had begun in 1958. The very nature of the planning made the point that the multiversity, as it then existed, was not perfect, was subject to variation and possible improvement. On these new campuses solutions were already being sought in 1958 to problems that were dramatically highlighted beginning with the fall of 1964.

I had hoped in this unwritten chapter to indicate how some of the emerging problems could be solved, how some of the needed changes could best be effectuated. That task was postponed until a later time and then undertaken under other auspices. These lectures would have been more complete and better balanced if the missing fourth chapter had been added in 1963; if more attention had then been given to the proper uses of the university in serving the wellbeing of students on campus and of mankind around the world; if the concluding section had treated with the relation of the university to the eternal search for Utopia.

5

ATTEMPTED REFORMS
THAT FAILED

Once again, much has happened to higher education and to the United States since these lectures were written in the early spring of 1963 and even since the 1972 postscript. To higher education: the student revolts, affirmative action and the Bakke case, the Higher Education Amendments of 1972 with vast new sums for student aid, universal access to higher education instead of the earlier mass access, a turn in the labor market against the college graduate, increasing middle-class hedonism among parents and its counterpart of "me-ism" among students, the first impacts of the demographic depression, and much else. To the United States: the loss of the war in Vietnam, Watergate, the oil crises, brought on by the Organization of Petroleum Exporting Countries (OPEC), and a series of recessions, the failure of our intervention in Iran, the reincarnation of the Cold War, the fading of the American dream of increasing affluence stretching out to the endless horizon, Reaganomics, and much else. Yet, and this is the central theme of this postscript, the American research university remains much the same. The Harvard of 1982 is not all that different from the Harvard of 1963, or the Berkeley of 1982 from that of 1963. Most of the rest of higher education has changed very substantially but, and partly because of this, as I shall note below, not the research university.

This slow change should not be so entirely surprising if one looks even briefly at the long trends of history. Heraclitus said that "nothing endures but change." About the university it might be said, instead, that "everything else changes, but the university mostly endures"—particularly in the United States. About eighty-five institutions in the Western world established by 1520 still exist in recognizable forms, with similar functions and with unbroken histories, including the Catholic church, the Parliaments of the Isle of Man, of Iceland, and of Great Britain, several Swiss cantons, and seventy universities. Kings that rule, feudal lords with vassals, and guilds with monopolies are all gone. These seventy universities, however, are still in the same locations with some of the same buildings, with professors and students doing much the same things, and with governance carried on in much the same ways. There have been many intervening variations on the ancient themes, it is true, but the eternal themes of teaching, scholarship, and service, in one combination or another, continue. Looked at from within, universities have changed enormously in the emphases on their several functions and in their guiding spirits, but looked at from without and comparatively, they are among the least changed of institutions.

How can this be so? Universities still turn out essentially the same products—members of the more ancient professions of theology, teaching, medicine and the law, and scholarship. The universities have not been subject to any major technological change as has industry and agriculture and transportation. The faculty members continue to operate as individual craftsmen.

Universities, traditionally, as with the churches, have had a degree of autonomy from political and economic control that is quite remarkable, partly because they have been protected by the upper classes, however constituted, at nearly all times in almost every type of society. They have, on occasion, through what has gone on within them, helped to change the world but have themselves been much less changed than most of the rest of the world.

The last two decades in the United States have been no exception to the general rule that the "attributes" of the university (as Spinoza said of God) "are eternal." There have been revolts and crises in these recent times, but the American university has come out of all this much as it went in. I speak here of the approximately 100 "research universities" in the nation, as defined in the Carnegie Classification, and particularly of the half of this number identified as Research Universities I.[1] The phenomenon to explain is not the changes that have taken place in the universities since about 1960 but the changes that have not taken place, to which I shall turn shortly. Some of the explanations for this paucity of change are these:

1. The research universities are part of a loose system of higher education. The great shift from mass to universal access to higher education was absorbed by the community colleges and by the comprehensive colleges and universities, not by the research universities, and particularly not by the Research Universities I. Total enrollments in the public community colleges alone increased ten times over between 1960 and 1980, from 400,000 to 4,000,000, and the percentage of all enrollments increased from 11 to 35, while the percentage of all enrollments in Research Universities I fell from nearly 20 to under 10 percent. This is the contrary of what happened, for example, in Italy, where massive new enrollments were dumped on the preexisting uni-

versities. The elite institutions in the United States remained elite; some became even more elite in their admission standards. The rest of the system absorbed the impacts of this enormous historic development. In the course of doing this, the rest of the system also accommodated all those new lesser professions and occupations that would also have diluted the universities. In particular, the one-time teachers' colleges became comprehensive colleges and universities with a vast added array of occupationally oriented programs. The community colleges and the comprehensive colleges and universities took on, even eagerly, the impacts of universal access to higher education.

2. The research universities are substantially independent from each other, each making its own adjustments. At the time of the student revolts, for example, some made more concessions to students than others, but each in its own way. Contrast this with the overall legislation on university governance that took place in France, Germany, the Netherlands, Sweden, and elsewhere. The American universities also pulled back from their concessions one at a time, and quietly. This was not so possible in Europe where legislation had been enacted.

3. These research universities have many sources of financial support—federal, state and private; and the federal and the private, in turn, are themselves quite diverse. Decline of one source could be, and usually was, offset by increase in another. The universities in the United Kingdom, under the Department of Education and Science and the University Grants Committee, on the contrary, rely mostly on a single source, and when disaster strikes, have no other place to turn, as happened in the early 1980's.

4. Almost regardless of what else is happening, society needs the highest skills and the best new knowledge, and, in the United States, the research university is the chief source of both. And

higher and higher premiums are being paid for the highest skills and the best new knowledge. The role of the research university becomes ever more important.

5. The faculties are substantially in control, and they are most conservative about their own affairs, never more so than when their own affairs are not going too well.

Nevertheless, there have been some changes:

1. Many universities are somewhat larger—some significantly so, including Ohio State, the University of Michigan, Michigan State University, and the University of Minnesota.

2. There has been some shift in the composition of the different categories of research universities (from 1963 to 1979), but not all that much (see Table 1). For example, four new universities entered the list of the top twenty recipients of federal funds for academic science (the University of California at San Diego, the University of California at San Francisco, Pennsylvania State University, and Washington University), and four dropped out at least temporarily (New York University, Ohio State University, the University of Rochester, and the University of Texas); but the other sixteen would have been among the leaders in research activity in 1950, and most of them also in 1920. Twelve of the fourteen original members of the Association of American Universities (established in 1900) are now in the top twenty as defined above. Once a reputation has been established, once a set of policies and academic standards has been set in place, once a sense of pride takes over—they all tend to perpetuate themselves. But there may be some changes by the year 2000 in the top twenty and certainly in the top fifty and the top hundred. Diverse geographical locations will be one explanation for change, leading either to more growth or to more decline in enrollments, which will conduce, in turn, to more chances for new endeavors and improvements in old programs or to the absence of such

Table 1   Institutions defined as Research Universities, 1963–1965
and 1976

Institution	1963–1965	1976
University of Alabama	X	
University of Arizona	X	X
University of Arkansas	X	X
Auburn University		X
Boston University	X	X
Brandeis University		X
Brown University	X	X
California Institute of Technology	X	X
University of California, Berkeley	X	X
University of California, Davis		X
University of California, Irvine		X
University of California, Los Angeles	X	X
University of California, San Diego	X	X
Carnegie-Mellon University	X	X
Case-Western Reserve University	X	X
Catholic University of America	X	X
University of Chicago	X	X
University of Cincinnati	X	X
Claremont University Center and Claremont Graduate School		X
Colorado State University	X	X
University of Colorado, Boulder	X	X
Columbia University	X	X
University of Connecticut		X
Cornell University	X	X
University of Denver	X	
Duke University	X	X
Emory University	X	X
Florida State University	X	X
University of Florida	X	X
Fordham University	X	
George Washington University	X	X
Georgetown University	X	X
Georgia Institute of Technology		X
University of Georgia	X	X

Table 1   (continued)

Institution	1963–1965	1976
Harvard University	X	X
University of Hawaii, Manoa		X
Howard University		X
University of Illinois, Urbana	X	X
Indiana State University, Bloomington	X	X
Iowa State University of Science and Technology	X	X
University of Iowa	X	X
Johns Hopkins University	X	X
Kansas State University of Agriculture and Applied Sciences	X	X
University of Kansas	X	X
University of Kentucky	X	X
Louisiana State University and A & M College, Baton Rouge	X	X
University of Maryland, College Park	X	X
Massachusetts Institute of Technology	X	X
University of Massachusetts, Amherst		X
University of Miami		X
Michigan State University	X	X
University of Michigan, Ann Arbor	X	X
University of Minnesota, Minneapolis-St. Paul	X	X
Mississippi State University		X
University of Missouri, Columbia	X	X
University of Nebraska	X	X
University of New Mexico		X
City University of New York Graduate School and University Center		X
New York University	X	X
State University of New York, Buffalo	X	X
State University of New York, Stony Brook	X	X
North Carolina State University, Raleigh	X	X
University of North Carolina, Chapel Hill	X	X

Institution	1963–1965	1976
Northwestern University	X	X
University of Notre Dame	X	
Ohio State University	X	X
Oklahoma State University	X	X
University of Oklahoma	X	X
Oregon State University		X
University of Oregon	X	X
Pennsylvania State University	X	X
University of Pennsylvania	X	X
University of Pittsburgh	X	X
Polytechnic Institute of Brooklyn	X	
Princeton University	X	X
Purdue University	X	X
Rensselaer Polytechnic Institute	X	
Rice University	X	
University of Rochester	X	X
Rockefeller University		X
Rutgers, The State University	X	X
St. Louis University		X
University of Southern California	X	X
Stanford University	X	X
Syracuse University	X	X
Temple University	X	X
University of Tennessee, Knoxville	X	X
Texas A & M University	X	X
University of Texas, Austin	X	X
Tufts University		X
Tulane University of Louisiana	X	X
Utah State University		X
University of Utah	X	X
Vanderbilt University	X	X
University of Vermont and State Agricultural College		X
Virginia Polytechnic Institute and State University		X
University of Virginia	X	X

Table 1   (continued)

Institution	1963–1965	1976
Washington State University	X	X
Washington University	X	X
University of Washington	X	X
Wayne State University	X	X
West Virginia University		X
University of Wisconsin, Madison	X	X
Yale University	X	X
Yeshiva University	X	X

Sources: For 1976, Carnegie Council on Policy Studies in Higher Education, *A Classification of Institutions of Higher Education, Revised Edition* (Berkeley, Calif., 1976). For 1963–1965, institutions were defined as research universities on the basis of the criteria of the Carnegie Council's 1976 classification.

chances. Another explanation will be the extent to which individual institutions make difficult selective changes in academic programs, building on strengths and eliminating weaknesses, or just act "across-the-board," as is comparatively easy to do. A third explanation will be the comparative strength of their professional schools, which (except for engineering schools) are usually strongest in the private institutions, as these professional areas continue to gain in comparative importance. In particular, there may come to be some new peaks of excellence, if strong and wise academic leadership is asserted, in the South and in the Mountain States where few now exist. All the additions to the list of Research Universities I from 1963 to 1979 (five in total) are in the South and the West.

3. Federal research funds for academic science have been spread more evenly around the country. When *The Uses of the University* was first written, the top twenty universities ("the primary

federal grant universities") received 50 percent of federal funds for academic science; today the figure is 40 percent. The top thirty now get 50 percent and the top forty receive 60 percent. This is quite legitimate, since scholarly competence has been spread over more institutions. It is how some of the other 40 or 50 percent of federal funds for academic science is spent that is troublesome, since it is distributed now to over 900 institutions as compared with under 800 in 1963, and often for political reasons. There have been no complaints about this from academic sources as long as there have been sufficient funds to go around, and, in fact, this wider distribution, however wasteful in results, has been supported as politically necessary to protect the support of the top forty or so institutions. The emphasis has shifted gradually, as I earlier feared it might, from "excellence" toward "balance." This shift may continue to take place.

4. A deficit of Ph.D.s in 1963 has turned to a surplus in 1982. The source of new Ph.D.s has changed substantially from 75 percent from the Research Universities I to 50 percent.

5. Professional fields have grown comparatively in enrollments, particularly engineering, business administration, and medicine, and the "academic" fields have declined proportionately. This means, among many other things, that the universities become more conservative in their politics both among students and faculty.

6. A higher proportion of students are women and minorities. But none of these is a fundamental change.

Fundamental Changes Attempted—And Failed

Academic reform.   Every American research university in the 1960's and 1970's engaged in one or more academic reforms, most of them in many. The same was true of most liberal arts colleges and most comprehensive colleges and universities, but much less so of community colleges. I speak here of "intended internally originated academic structural change"[2] when I use the words "academic reform."

The two great periods of academic change in American higher education were (1) after the Civil War with the land-grant movement and the modernizing efforts of Eliot at Harvard, White at Cornell, Gilman at Johns Hopkins, and others, and (2) in the 1960's. In between there were minor efforts at change aimed mostly at a return to "general education," as those made under Lowell at Harvard. The 1870's and the 1960's had at least two things in common: a spurt of growth in enrollments that made additions of new faculty and new programs much easier, and new surges forward in national efforts in which higher education could participate.

The national efforts in the 1870's were to industrialize rapidly and to settle the whole continental United States, the latter of which meant new agricultural crops in new areas. Higher education became a source of science and technology, of engineers and farm agents, going far beyond the earlier classical education for the historic professions of teaching, medicine, the law, and the ministry. The national efforts in the 1960's were to advance science and technology after Sputnik and to provide more equality of opportunity for members of lower-income groups and for minorities and for women. Higher education intensified its existing emphasis on science and technology (and this involved few changes), and, within the system as a whole, moved from mass access to universal access to higher education and opened up several professional fields to women and minorities. The national efforts in both the 1870's and 1960's were generally successful, least so in the area of provision of greater equality of opportunity in the 1960's, and at both times higher education played a constructive role.

The internal academic changes that accompanied these forward movements were generally fruitful after the Civil War but
generally not in the 1960's. I note this latter fact with sadness.[3]
I had high hopes for academically inspired changes and participated actively in their promotion, particularly as president of the
University of California in the creation of the Santa Cruz campus
(about which Gerald Grant and David Riesman once wrote that
"no university . . . has achieved a more vibrant pluralism in the
forms of intellectual, social, and aesthetic experiences for undergraduates,"[4]) and as chairman of the Carnegie Commission and
later the Carnegie Council on Higher Education, which made so
many proposals for academic changes, especially in a report
entitled *Less Time, More Options.*[5] I also watched the failure of
the Tussman and Strawberry College experiments at Berkeley
and, as a member of the governing board of Swarthmore, the
only partially effective efforts to maintain and restore the honors
program at that college—the great innovation of Frank Aydelotte
in the 1920's. I know of no inventory of intentional academic
changes of the 1960's that shows their survival rate,[6] but I would
judge that about 90 percent were discontinued or so attenuated
as to disappoint their authors; but then their authors, under the
prevailing circumstances, often expected too much.

Why? The essential conservatism of faculty members about
their own affairs is certainly one reason. This is abetted by the
tendency to rely on consensus and on the opinions of the older
members of any academic group in making decisions. Also, there
are no rewards to the faculty members who seek academic innovation, only the burden of long, drawn out, and often disap-
pointing consultation. Most academic reforms are, in fact, initiated by students, who are notoriously inconstant in their efforts,
partly because of their rapid turnover and their responsiveness
to current fads, and by administrators, who are usually, except
in new endeavors, such as a new campus, restrained by conven-

tion and by faculty committees in participating actively in academic affairs. Also, adaptations over past decades and even centuries may well have found the best way of doing things, the tried and true. And, more fundamentally, there often may be no best way, only different ways.[7] Half a dozen ways may be equally effective or ineffective, so there is no strong argument for change. The big research university is particularly impervious to structural changes.

But, I think, there are three more reasons why the attempted changes of the 1960's largely failed. Many changes at that time in American history attracted faculty members and students who, by their nature—often disaffected and disenchanted as they were with academic and political life—would not let anything work well, particularly somebody else's attempted reforms. Reforms were killed by the customers of reform; reforms were stung to death by the hornets they attracted. The reforms of the 1870's, by contrast, attracted the upwardly mobile and docile children of farmers and immigrants, not the sliders down the meritocratic pyramid of success that had been built up by the 1960's.

Another reason is that the changes of the 1960's moved mostly in directions that faculty members by and large opposed. Such changes often called for more time, often much more time, spent with students, and a broader coverage of subject matters, as in "integrated" programs. The changes of the 1870's moved in ways many faculty members (but by no means all) liked—toward specialized courses, self-governing departments, graduate work, student electives, research.[8] The new faculty members, and particularly the new scientists, were avid supporters, even though the older classicists kicked and screamed all the way.

The changes of the 1870's had a central theme—enhancement of expertise, of science and scholarship. The attempted changes of the 1960's were oriented not toward the advancement of knowledge but toward improved environments for undergraduate students, usually in ways that cost faculty members in time and attention and emotion. Faculty members at Santa Cruz often complained of how time was taken from their research and how their emotions were drained by contact with students. The changes of the 1870's liberated faculty members; the changes of the 1960's tied them down to their offices and to their undergraduate students. The changes of the 1870's liberated faculty members from *in loco parentis* and those of the 1960's enslaved them again. It was the students of the 1960's who wanted *in loco parentis* in terms of personal attention but hated it in terms of impersonal rules enforced by the dean of students—the form it had come to take after the 1870's.

The one most successful academic change advocated by the Carnegie Commission, which coined the phrase and argued its merits, was the "stop-out," in the form of readily available leaves of absence of students. "Stop-outs" were troublesome to registrars and housing supervisors but not to faculty. The academic changes of the 1960's originated in student bull-sessions and in the minds and hearts of administrators who listened to students; they died in the faculty clubs. An exception was the reform at M.I.T. which brought undergraduate students into participation with faculty members on research projects. This reform originated with faculty members and paralleled faculty interests.

A third reason for the difference between the 1870's and the 1960's was that the national thrusts of the 1870's required fundamental academic changes, specifically the creation of the modern university with its emphasis on research and occupational training. The national thrusts of the 1960's, however, could be accommodated within the existing structures; they did not require fundamental changes. Additionally, presidents, who were the great agents of change, had much more power in the 1870's than in the 1960's, and faculties much less.

Some changes of the 1960's were based not on academic but

on political concerns and were forced into practice by student pressure, changes such as programs in Black studies, Native American studies, and Hispanic studies. Faculty members generally never liked them; in fact, barely tolerated them. Born in the passion of student activism, they have mostly withered, or at least wilted, in the silent embrace of faculty committees.

I introduced this section with the phrase "intended internally originated academic structural change" and have suggested that the attempted reform movement was a flame that burned brightly for a while and then flickered out, its extinction mourned by only a few. I count myself among those few. But there were academic changes on a major scale that originated in the marketplace external to educational policy considerations, and these "popular reforms" succeeded where the "telic" reforms failed.[9] These changes consisted of the fundamental shift from liberal to vocational studies,[10] and, within vocational studies, from one field to another—with engineering, for example, going up and down in its attractiveness to students like a yo-yo. Business administration and the paramedical specialties were the great gainers. The composition of instructional effort, measured field by field, must have changed by at least one-third over two decades. This was a revolution of major proportions in what faculty members taught, what students studied, what librarians bought, which departments faded or grew in importance, what kinds of classrooms and laboratories were built, and where they were located on campus. In American higher education, changes influenced by the market are accepted in a way that reforms originating in concerns for educational policy are not. An appropriate emblem for the American college might be the traditional open book, but lying on a sales counter.[11]

The Golden Age of the 1960's and 1970's, because of growth, was a comparatively favorable period for academic idealism;

some basic improvements could then have been made, but the opportunities were largely missed.

Reconstitution of the university into a direct agent of social reform.   Colleges and universities throughout American history have been looked upon as instruments of social reform. Harvard was founded in part to "advance learning and perpetuate it to Posterity; dreading to leave an illiterate Ministery to the Churches, when our present Ministers shall lie in the Dust."[12] In the 1960's and 1970's there were two major efforts to use the university deliberately to change society.

One such effort was by the federal government to increase equality of opportunity. This was done, in part, by offering grants to college students based upon their comparative ability to pay and, in part, by forcing colleges and universities to change their policies to admit more minorities and women as faculty members. Consequently, many more minorities and women have attended institutions of higher education, but most of them come from the higher income groups. Progress in increasing attendance from low-income groups has been meager (see Table 2). It has been easier to change policies and practices and preferences that make distinctions on the basis of sex and race than on income group. Attendance can be made more possible, but the choice to attend remains voluntary, and academic ability and interest are not equally distributed across income groups.[13]

The hope that many of us had that higher education by 1976 would draw equal proportions of students with high academic ability from all levels of family incomes has been disappointed.[14] This remains a still remote but still achievable goal. And, in my judgment, much of the progress that has been made has been because of the new temper of the times and the aroused conscience of the academic community, and little because of direct federal intervention.

Table 2   Composition of students and faculty in institutions of
higher education, 1960 and late 1970's, in percentages

	1960	Late 1970's
Women		
Undergraduate enrollment	38.0[a]	51.2 (1979)[b]
Graduate enrollment	29.0[a]	48.9 (1979)[b]
Faculty and other professional staff	22.0[c]	24.8 (1978)[d]
Racial and ethnic groups (includes		
Black, Asian, and Native American)		
Undergraduate enrollment	6.6[e]	13.0 (1978)[f]
Graduate and professional enrollment	6.1[e]	7.8 (1978)[f]
Faculty	—	8.8 (1977)[g]
Black faculty	3.0[h]	4.4 (1979)[g]
Low-income students		
Students from families in bottom		
one-fifth of national income		
distribution	8.7[i]	14.0 (1979)[j]

a. National Center for Education Statistics, *Projections of Education
Statistics to 1975–76* (Washington, D.C.: U.S. Government Printing Office,
1966), Tables 11 and 12.

b. National Center for Education Statistics, *Fall Enrollment in Higher
Education, 1979* (Washington, D.C.: U.S. Government Printing Office, 1980),
Tables 2 and 4.

c. Calculated from National Center for Education Statistics, *Digest of
Educational Statistics, 1968* (Washington, D.C.: U.S. Government Printing
Office, 1968), Table 100.

d. *Digest of Education Statistics, 1979,* p. 101. Women constituted 25.9
percent of full-time instructional faculty in 1979–80 (National Center for
Education Statistics, "Women Faculty Still Lag in Salary and Tenure for the
1979–80 Academic Year," Early Release, NCES 80-342).

e. United States Census of Population, 1960, Subject Reports, *School
Enrollment,* Final Report PC(2)-5A.

f. Calculated from National Center for Education Statistics, *Fall Enrollment
in Higher Education, 1978* (Washington, D.C.: U.S. Government Printing
Office, 1979), Table 29.

g. "Higher Education Staff Information—EEO-6," Report of the U.S. Equal
Employment Opportunity Commission, 1977.

h. Institute for the Study of Educational Policy, *Affirmative Action for Blacks in Higher Education: A Report* (Washington, D.C.: Howard University, 1978), p. 25.

i. U.S. Bureau of the Census. *Current Population Reports*, Series P-20, No. 183, "Characteristics of Students and Their Colleges, October 1966" (Washington, D.C., 1969), Table 2; and *Current Population Reports*, Series P-60, No. 105, "Money Income in 1975 of Families and Persons in the United States" (Washington, D.C., 1977), Table 13.

j. U.S. Bureau of the Census. *Current Population Reports*, Series P-20, No. 346, "Population Characteristics: School Enrollment—Social and Economic Characteristics of Students: October 1978" (Washington, D.C., October 1979), Table 25; and *Current Population Reports*, Series P-60, No. 120, Table 5.

All those billions of federal dollars in student aid did more to raise college attendance than to change its composition in terms of source of students by level of family income. It may have had a good political effect, however, by indicating the public's concern for a commitment to equality of opportunity—by creating a situation where lack of attendance was more a matter of choice than of necessity. It brought more money into higher education. It also subsidized middle-income hedonism by reducing financial burdens on middle-income parents.

Progress in participation of minorities and women at the faculty level again has been slow, but faster for women than for minorities. The as-yet-smaller sizes of pools of trained people is one reason, but another is that federal programs got off to a late start, after the massive new hirings of the 1960's were past. Still another reason is the difficulty governmental agencies have in challenging the autonomy of universities and their meritocratic standards—and of course prejudice on campus plays a role.

The second effort to use the university to change society was by students with some faculty support. It sought to use the campus as a staging ground to "reconstitute" society through political discussion, demonstration, and protest. The major targets were racial injustice and the Vietnam war, but also environmental pollution and nuclear power, among others. In no case did the students initiate these issues; they did, however, draw each issue more insistently to national attention. In my judgment, the student use of the colleges and universities was largely ineffective. Blacks quickly rejected the proffered leadership of their movement by the upper-class whites on campus. The federal administration, and particularly President Nixon, adroitly used student protest as one way of temporarily increasing acceptance of continuing the war in Vietnam, by encouraging the backlash of public opinion against the students. And, in any event, students abruptly abandoned their efforts in the summer and fall of 1970. The student effort was divisive on campus and off, and costly in morale internally and in support externally. Students generally have been more effective in getting what they have wished by individually voting with their feet, as they choose what they want and do not want by way of courses, programs, and types of colleges, than by expressing themselves with their voices collectively. I believe that student political effort was not bound inherently to be so ineffective. It was ineffective because of excessive and alienating rhetoric, and the occasional use of force. A more reasoned, persuasive approach might have worked. The student lobbies of the 1970's have, by way of comparison, been effective.

Higher education, however, does reform, or at least change, society indirectly in many ways. New knowledge is one of the great moving forces in our society. The more education that people have, the more liberal their attitudes are on issues such as race, sexual practices, and abortion; the more likely they are to be well informed about public issues and to vote in elections;

the more likely they are to take better care of their health, to act prudently as investors, to act effectively as consumers; the more likely they are to accept and to adapt to change.[15] Styles of life are affected. The counter-culture did not originate on campus, but it was avidly embraced there and distributed from there in the writings of faculty members and the actions of students and graduates. The "new breed," as Dan Yankelovich identifies it, is essentially defined by acceptance of the counter-culture and now constitutes, it is said, about half of the American population as against the largely non-college "old breed."[16]

The direct use of the university as an instrument of social reform has had a recent record, depending on source, purpose, and methods, that has ranged from partially effective to counterproductive. The presence of institutions of higher education in society, on the other hand, has many fundamental long-term consequences. The presence of the university carrying out its normal functions changes society fundamentally, but the attempted manipulation of the university, for the sake of specific political reforms, changes the university for the worse more than it changes society for the better.

Changes in governance.   I once thought that alternative modes of governance had substantial significance in American higher education. I fought very hard for a system of voluntary advisory coordination when we were setting up the Master Plan in California in 1960. The differential consequences of alternative forms of governance has been an assumption of many others as well; witness the many books and articles on the subject and the many battles fought during the past twenty years. I began questioning my assumption when a study financed by the Carnegie Commission on the impacts on performance of different forms of state coordination, from voluntary to compulsory, showed no significant variations in performance.[17] I would now advance the conclusion that, within the range of alternatives considered in the United States,[18] forms of governance make some difference but not as much as often supposed.

There have been many battles over issues of governance in recent years: over federal intervention, particularly in behalf of affirmative action; over the creation of a federal department of education, which the Carnegie Council opposed but which I now think was not worth the cost of opposition; over forms of state-wide coordination; over the creation of multi-campus systems and the distribution of authority within them;[19] over the placement of students on committees—but they seldom attend, or participate erratically if they do; over "participatory democracy" more generally, which I define as giving each identifiable group not only a voice but also a veto; over collective bargaining by faculty, which has done more to generate new rules than to raise the real income of faculty members.

What has been the result of all these battles won and lost? More formal rules, certainly, but there were always a good many, and all of society is moving that way; more internal and external reports to be made, but, again, this is a universal trend; a lessened sense of attachment within the campus community and of institutional autonomy, but, here again, all of society is becoming more integrated; a more conservative, more cumbersome, more time-consuming system of governance. It is ironic that participatory democracy, with its emphasis that all the "people" should be consulted and all groups have a veto, which was supposed to result in more radical decisions, in more speedy and more responsive actions, has meant, instead, more veto groups, less action, more commitment to the status quo—the status quo is the only solution that cannot be vetoed. Instead of releasing the pent-up energy of the masses, participatory democracy has confirmed the power of special-interest groups to stop changes they do not like; and, it has weakened campus leadership—few administrative heads are now raised above the parapets. Where have the leaders gone? They have gone where they have also gone in corporations, unions, and government. The two most serious consequences of changes in the governance of higher education, I believe, are the last two: participatory democracy and weakened leadership—both negative from the point of view of the continued dynamics of American higher education.

But does it matter? The internal life of higher education goes on much the same: the teaching, the formation of the curriculum, the research, the public service. How could this be? I think there is a good explanation. Most decisions are really made outside the formal system of governance, are made in more informal, less bureaucratic ways. The more visible superstructure of governance is less important than the less visible infrastructure. Most decisions about teaching, about curriculum, about research topics and methods, about amount and form of public service are made by individual faculty members. Most decisions made about majors selected, courses taken, and time spent on study are made by individual students. And intense competition among institutions of higher education, public versus private and public versus public, means that all are seeking optimum solutions; none can afford to lag too far behind. Decisions made in these three ways—by individual faculty members, by individual students, and in response to external competition through market pressures—are the most accepted, the least contested, and considered to be the most legitimate.

Looking only at what is happening to the formal superstructure of governance is like looking only at a part of the whole—important, but not all that decisive. What are faculty members deciding individually? How are students voting with their feet? What does interinstitutional competition compel? These are more essential questions than what form a coordinating council should take or whether or not there should be a federal department of education. This is why several different forms of formal super-structure may not have significantly different impacts on comparative results.

But I would still argue for giving leadership a better chance to exert itself. Most successful new policies in higher education have come from the top. We need to reverse the denigration of leadership. Leadership does matter. It was denigrated by students, by faculty, by trustees in the late 1960's and early 1970's. In the spring of 1969, I was invited to attend a meeting of the Association of American Universities. I had not been to a meeting for two-and-one-half years. I said to the executive secretary that I seemed to know only about half of the nearly fifty presidents who were there. He replied that this was easily explained—anyone who held office by the end of that academic year would be halfway up the seniority list. Presidents were used like Kleenex. The institutions survived, but their leaders did not. Yet in a time of troubles, as then loomed and now looms ahead, leaders are more needed but are harder to get to serve and to keep. To the list of presidential attributes I gave in the original lectures, I would now add the ability to withstand the frustrations from all of the checks and balances, and the criticism from all of the more active and vocal participants; that is, the possession of nerves like sewer pipes.

My thesis is that, within the confines of the changes in the governance of universities considered in the United States, and given the heavy emphasis on individually made decisions by faculty members and students and the active competition among institutions, one specific arrangement in governance versus another has minor implications for what actually happens in a university (although processes may be made more time consuming and more personally disagreeable), with the two exceptions of the arrangements for and the spirit of participatory democracy and the reduced effectiveness of leadership. Many battles have been fought over relatively minor alternatives while less attention has been directed toward these two critical issues. Let me say, however, that this conclusion has been reached after directly observing only about thirty years of history. Over a longer span of time some alternatives that now appear to have about the same impact on actual results (such as whether students sit as members of faculty committees or not) might turn out to have greater significance than I have given them here—for example, at a time of a major crisis.

The massive long-run developments in governance have been from dominance by the board of trustees beginning with 1636, to dominance by the president after 1870, to dominance by the faculty after 1920, to present and greater prospective dominance by the student market.

The three fundamental changes attempted over the past twenty years have largely failed. Academic reform was overwhelmed by faculty conservatism. Efforts to turn the university into a direct instrument for social change were thwarted by institutional autonomy when tried from the outside, and by the inconsistencies between efforts at political assault on society and the continuing conduct of the academic purposes of the campus when tried from within. Changes in formal governance have generally made little difference and, when they did, mostly for the worse. All that effort, all that passion, all that turmoil was mostly for naught, but it was also mostly inevitable given the conditions of the times.

What Have We Learned or Relearned?

How strong the modern American university is; how well it fits its environment; how resilient it is to attacks; how little subject it is to fundamental changes; how it can survive and advance in the 1980's and 1990's as it did in the 1960's and 1970's.

How important to the university are its autonomy and its financing from a series of independent sources; how significant that there is no one master but rather a series of fifty states and of many independent private boards.

How protected the university is, surrounded by so many other types of institutions of higher education that shield it from overwhelming numbers of students and from educational duties not compatible with its central functions.

How important are the boards of trustees of American universities to their autonomy and to their dynamics, and how important it is that these boards be composed of individuals devoted to the welfare of their institutions, well informed about their affairs, highly sensitive to the special nature and spirit of academic institutions, and capable of good long-term judgment, even in the midst of severe current pressures.

How conservative the faculty is within its departments and its committees, and how volatile it is en masse under stress, when it may do, and sometimes has done, almost any wild thing; how effective it is individually in intellectual pursuits, yet how it can collectively overreact in more emotional matters. How faculty moods change, as from too optimistic in the 1960's to too pessimistic in the 1970's, and how the universities carry on a much steadier course than these shifting moods would imply.

How volatile the students are in their choices of fields of study, their attachment to political causes and instruments, in their styles of life. I once said in the 1950's as Chancellor at Berkeley that the great administrative problems of the day were sex for the students, athletics for the alumni, and parking for the faculty; but it could better be said now that the problems are, instead, athletics for the students who have gone "straight," sex for the professors with some of whom the counter-culture still finds support, and parking for the alumni as they return for their refresher courses.

How attached are the alumni to the university they once knew; how the conservative alumni are mostly the more loyal and active among the alumni; and how easily they can be aroused by change in a liberal direction, as they have been at Yale, Princeton, and Berkeley.

How strong is the underlying public support for higher education; but how strong are the temporary public reactions to departures from what is expected of higher education in its conduct.

How steady the states are in their support of higher education. Average real state expenditures per full-time student in public institutions remained essentially the same from 1968 to 1977, despite all that was happening in the United States and in higher education.[20] And how unsteady is federal support by purpose, as it shifts from one emphasis to another, and in amount.

How great is the role of aggressive governors for good (Rockefeller in New York) or for ill (Reagan in California), but how governors come and go.

How invulnerable the research university is to enrollment changes in higher education as a whole, since its level of enrollment is largely subject to its own control.

How necessary the American research university is to the advancement of research and the preparation of highly skilled personnel, both in ever greater demand. How central the American research universities have become to worldwide academic life at the highest levels.

How the troubles ahead, particularly demographic depression and budget restrictions, will not greatly affect the research universities, much as they may impinge on other segments of higher education.

How the American research university will be even more essential to American society in 1990 or 2000 than it is today or was in 1960.

How the lessons we have learned from the past will continue to be applicable for the foreseeable future, because the universities change so slowly and so little.

I conclude this postscript as I began the original lectures, by saying that the research university in America still has a long way to go.

6

COMMENTARIES
ON THE GOLDEN AGE OF
THE RESEARCH UNIVERSITY

The half century 1940–1990 was a largely golden age for the research university in the United States. I set forth below, as of 1994, some reflections on what I earlier wrote about this period, from the current perspective that some major developments now taking place may signal a new age.

Preface 1963: A Hinge of History

The "hinge of history" can be seen even more dramatically in 1994 than in 1963. Federal research funds have risen about four times over since 1960—the federal grant research university was then only in its infancy, and student enrollment for all institutions of higher education has gone up about five times over in the same period—universal access has become a reality. (For the full period since 1940, the increases have been more than twenty-five times over for federal research funds and nearly ten times over for student enrollment.)

NOTATIONS

1. A whole series of studies by economists since 1963 has shown that increases in economic productivity are based, in a general range of 40–60 percent, on "advances in knowledge."

2. The role of the universities in "advances in knowledge" is suggested by the amount of federal R&D funds (in constant 1982–1984 dollars and without university-managed federal laboratories) awarded to universities in millions of dollars:

1930	$ 135
1940	310
1953	515
1963	2,485
1968	4,510
1973	4,470
1978	4,690
1983	5,010
1988	6,925
1993	7,995

Data for 1930 and 1940 are for all federal funds, not only R&D but mostly R&D.

3. Teaching hours of research university faculty members have decreased by about one-half, from nine per week to four-and-one-half.[1] Nine hours, with preparation, advising, committee work, examinations, and so forth, makes close to a "full load" (forty hours per week) in areas with constant new information to absorb. At that level of teaching, most research was "on-the-side" (marginal hours and "overtime" during the week, weekends, summers, sabbaticals) and not the main concentration of effort. At the new level of teaching, research has become the largest single component of the total endeavors. It should also be noted that the largest subsidy by universities and by the states to "federal R&D" is reduced teaching loads, which are across-

the-board and not just in those areas of "academic science" that federal R&D supports. Research universities shift resources to support federal R&D projects in other ways as well.

4. In 1963, I noted the "unprecedented proportion of the population" going to colleges and universities. Total enrollment (on a head-count basis) has been as follows in millions of students:

1930	1.1
1940	1.5
1950	2.5
1960	3.2
1970	7.1
1980	12.1
1990	13.7

Since they were concentrated on the research universities, the original Godkin Lectures were mostly concerned with the impacts of more attention to searching for new knowledge. The second great simultaneous appearance of unprecedented numbers of students more affected the community colleges and what came to be called "comprehensive colleges and universities." I have elsewhere considered in some detail this second aspect as we moved from mass to universal access to higher education.[2]

Research universities now account for about 20 percent of all students and faculty members in American higher education, and 3 percent of all institutions.

The Idea of the University

In the original lecture on this topic, I first set forth the three models (British, German, American) of a university that were combined in the modern "multiversity," and each with more or less equal status. Since 1963, one of these models has lost ground—the British or "liberal knowledge" for undergraduates model, which has also declined in Britain. This decline was not so clear in 1963, but it was inherent in the changing context. By 1963, the federal government, initially largely as an anti-depression action, had greatly aided the building of residence halls and student union buildings on the British model of a residential campus for undergraduates, and the "Hutchins' College" at Chicago and the "Red Book" at Harvard were still much discussed as means of reviving "liberal knowledge" for undergraduates.

Since 1963, however, "liberal knowledge" has been in retreat, greatly mourned but not even slightly revived, giving way to vocational and professional studies, as well as to greater and greater specialization within the arts and sciences; and "educational policy" is even less of a concern for most faculty members. Largely non-residential institutions, particularly community colleges and comprehensive colleges and universities, have, in terms of numbers of students, become more dominant as universal access has particularly impacted them, and as liberal arts colleges (many of which have turned "comprehensive") enroll a smaller proportion of students. The German (research) and American (service) models have advanced comparatively in influence. Overall there is less emphasis on what the Carnegie Commission called the "developmental growth of the individual student,"[3] to which the British model was so devoted—on what Pattison in England in the 1850s called making "a man."[4]

Second, I discussed the impacts on traditional forms of governance of the introduction of more "public authority" and of more separations between and within student and faculty groupings. I have since suggested that academic governance might best be viewed as the interactions among a series of loosely bound "estates," as in pre-revolutionary France, with each estate having a separate constituency, its own form (or forms) of decision-making, and its own spheres of control and/or influence.[5] (In the original Godkin Lectures, I used the term "nations" instead of "estates" with reference to the "nations" that loosely constituted the University of Bologna and some other early universities. I have sometimes thought an alternative designation might be "boutiques," as at Bloomingdale's.) These estates are associated together, sometimes with looser and sometimes with tighter bonds, but they do not together clearly constitute an organization with a single purpose and a monolithic hierarchical administration. The multiversity gives rise to multifractionated governance. By advancing, in my discussion in the original lecture, from purposes and functions to governance, I implied a causal connection between them but did not make it explicit that the multiversity inherently meant a more pluralistic form of governance, that the former led to the latter: multiple purposes and functions to multiple distributions of power.

Third, I turned to presidential leadership. I noted that the "giants" of the past were associated with the revolutionary development of the research university and with the attempted counterrevolutions against it (as by Lowell and Hutchins). However, without a revolution and without counterrevolutions, there were no longer such great visions for presidential giants to promote. Such revolutions or attempted counterrevolutions as there have been in more recent times have found their "giants" more in public figures in Washington (as in Conant, Bush, and Compton),[6] or in radical students and faculty members on campus. The multiversity led to multiple locations for leadership, with the president as the principal communicator and consensus-seeker among the many leaders, sharing everything except ultimate public relations responsibility.

Thus the logic of the situation was this: pluralistic purposes and functions led to pluralistic forms of governance, and pluralistic forms of governance led to the fractionated presidency. This was inherent in what I said but never set forth boldly as a chain of causation.

Fourth, I implied but never said directly that the campus itself was a potential casualty of this course of development. The Academy of Plato, the Lyceum of Aristotle, and the Oxford of Newman all were and had to be campuses. "Liberal knowledge" required that all (or at least most) essential subjects be studied in association with each other, and that all teachers and all students discuss them with each other. But research institutes can be separated from one another as they often have been, as in Germany, France, and Russia, and can even be separated from graduate students; although, I believe, there can be major costs in doing so. Newman, as I noted in my lecture, had written, "I do not see why a University should have any students—if its object were scientific and philosophical discovery." "Service," as in extension services and consulting, can also easily be located off-campus; but, once again, with substantial costs. Professional training can be located all over town, as in Rome and many Latin American cities. Libraries with books no longer have a monopoly on storage and retrieval of information; face-to-face communication has a lesser monopoly as a means of personal interaction. Faculty members and students can and do more easily commute over longer distances. It is now possible to teach concurrently in New York City and State College (Pennsylvania) and even in Paris and Columbia, as, on occasion, has happened.

The operation of the nerve system of academic life is now more and more dependent on computer terminals and facsimile machines (I have often thought that the "fax tank" is replacing the "think tank"), and less and less on face-to-face contact. This saddens me—colder mechanical contacts versus warmer biological interactions. My emotional attachment is still to the Swarthmore of the early 1930s. At the same time I was describing at Harvard in 1963 the more mechanistic "multiversity," I was working hard to establish a more organic series of "cluster colleges" at Santa Cruz[7] and to hold down the size of the campuses throughout the University of California. The terminology employed ("multiversity") turned out to be a more accurate description of reality than the latter efforts (the cluster colleges) turned into realized utopian reforms.

The general campus as a social environment is better suited for horizontal contacts among generalists; the individual, separated disciplines for vertical contacts among single-subject specialists. Thus the campus is better oriented toward internal relations, and the disciplines better toward external contacts with funding agencies, with practicing professionals, with academic journals, with pay-for-service clients. The president can *lead* in horizontal relations but, at best, can only *facilitate* vertical relations.

The traditional presidency was mostly campus based. It was primarily concerned with undergraduate students, with individual staff members, with alumni, with the local community, and with individual sources of general financial support. The disciplinary specialists of today mostly go around the president on their way to their own public funding sources, to publication opportunities, to purchasers of services. Increasing numbers of faculty members are less attached to the general campus and more attached to their individual disciplines; and the role of the president in their lives is less and less like that of a dominant Nicholas Murray Butler at Columbia or a Robert Gordon Sproul at California. The campus as primary (even sole) community of attachment gives way to the discipline—the cloister to the airport lounge and to computer and fax terminals, or at least to the two in tandem as co-primary communities.

Academic contacts in the Academy and the Lyceum were, presumably, mostly horizontal among persons with common interests and similar points of view. Academic contacts within and outside the multiversity are by now more vertical within narrower and narrower specialties. There are advantages to both systems. The horizontal is better for undergraduate students seeking a general education, for scholars seeking inspiration from contacts with other bodies of information and other methodologies, and for those interested in policy-making that deals with full-bodied reality. The vertical is better for straight-line advances within the specialty for the advanced student, as well as for the scholar seeking quicker and more frequent publication.

Too little thought, I think, has been given to what is happening and how to react to it. Should we let nature take its course with vertical contacts steadily replacing horizontal? Or should we set up (or preserve) mechanisms reserved for horizontal contacts by separating the college from the university, as Hutchins sought to do at Chicago? Or should we advance the process by splitting up the university even more into independent institutes, as in the German Max Planck Gesellschaft? Or should we try to find ways for the two approaches to coexist and to complement each other, as in the Quadrangle (Faculty) Club at Chicago and the various committees there that advance cross-disciplinary fields of study, or as at the London School of Economics (and other British institutions) with a common lounge for faculty members and graduate students, or as with the attempted colleges at the University of California at Santa Cruz and several of the newer British universities? Or should we encourage more ORUs (organized research units) to be actively composed of faculty members on a cross-disciplinary basis? Individual faculty members on their own can and do, of course, seek out intellectual contacts across departmental lines. Certainly one of the more perplexing issues of the intellectual world is how to make best use of both the horizontal and the vertical approaches to advancing and imparting knowledge.

My own conviction is that contacts, whether horizontal or vertical, are not best carried on by mechanical means alone; and, thus, that faculty opposition to the new technology as the preferred means of teaching is not just a Luddite response. Direct person-to-person contacts enhance motivation on both sides, better convey non-verbal information, offer improved opportunities to question and challenge, adjust to individual variations in depth of knowledge and rates of absorption of new information, and improve feedback generally.

Thus, in these several ways, what is happening to (1) purposes; (2) governance; (3) the presidency; and (4) the life of the campus is all intertwined together: to understand one, it is necessary to understand all.

The "Idea of the University" continues to evolve slowly and unevenly—not at all in some areas and rapidly in others.

James Bryce, in his 1914 edition of *The American Commonwealth*,[8] wrote as follows:

1. That there were about 10 or 15 universities "if we define a university as a place" where the "fullest and most exact knowledge of the times is given in a range of subjects covering all the great departments of intellectual life" (p. 715). (Today there are 125 "research universities" and another 110 "doctoral granting institutions.")

2. That the president held an "almost monarchical position." He was "a leading figure in the State, perhaps even in the Na-

tion." "No persons in the country . . . are better known, and certainly none are more respected" (pp. 718 and 748).

3. That "the conception of a general liberal education" is "insufficiently valued and imperfectly realized," whereas "practical subjects" are "unduly strong" (p. 761).

4. That "nowhere in the world do University teachers feel more strongly that the first object of their devotion is Truth" (p. 762).

5. That the university in America is "one of the most powerful and pervasive forces working for good in the country" (p. 762).

Bryce's observations are a benchmark from which to measure what has changed and how much.

NOTATIONS

1. I have since found another precedent for my use of the word "multiversity": Henry Adams, in *The Education of Henry Adams,* wrote about what he called the "multiverse,"[9] as did William James at a later date.

2. Abraham Flexner, as early as 1908, noted that the campus was becoming a series of separatist endeavors: departments "no longer all revolve around a central sun; they do not even freely interact"; they merely "live side by side."[10]

3. Immanuel Kant, even earlier, in 1798, had observed that the university was dissolving into "the conflict of the faculties,"[11] specifically theology (revelation) versus philosophy (reason), and more generally the "higher faculties" versus the "lower faculties." The academic world was losing its unity—and perhaps much earlier than 1798, beginning with the Reformation.

The Realities of the Federal Grant University

The American research grant university has been an enormous intellectual success, particularly in the sciences: Since 1950, when the development of federal research grant universities was in its infancy, 55 percent of all Nobel and Fields (mathematics) prizes have been awarded to scholars resident in the United States; in the 1980s, 50 percent of all citations in leading scientific journals around the world were to members of the same group; in 1990, 50 percent of all patents registered in the United States were of U.S. origin; and by 1990, the United States had 180,000 graduate students from foreign nations, clearly making it the world center of graduate study.

In 1987, Henry Rosovsky, former Dean of Arts and Sciences at Harvard, could write:

> In these days when foreign economic rivals seem to be surpassing us in one field after another, it may be reassuring to know that there is one vital industry where America unquestionably dominates the world: higher education. Between two-thirds and three-quarters of the world's best universities are located in the United States. This fact has been ignored by the many recent critics of higher education in America. (We also are home to a large share of the world's worst colleges and universities, but that is beside the point.)
>
> What other sector of our economy can make a similar statement? There are baseball, football, and basketball teams—but that pretty much exhausts the list. No one has suggested that today America is home to two-thirds of the best steel mills, automobile factories, chip manufacturers, banks, or government agencies. Our position at the upper end of the quality scale in higher education is unusual, may be a special national asset, and needs to be explained.
>
> In higher education, "made in America" still is the finest label. My only advice is to add "handle with care," lest we too descend to the level of most other American industrial performance.[12]

Not since Italy in the early centuries of the rise of universities in western Europe has any single nation so dominated intellectual life.

The success has been enormous.

The growth has been enormous.

Institutional costs, however, have also been substantial. Some impacts have been moving in the same directions I identified in 1963:

1. There is less attention to undergraduate teaching—with teaching loads of faculty members having fallen by about half, with greater use of teaching assistants, with increased class sizes, and with more "team teaching," where more than one faculty member claims credit for the same course.

2. The "balance" of research endeavors has continued to move toward human health and industrial and military advances—priorities set at the federal level.

3. Some faculty members are even more oriented toward federal funding and other contacts external to the campus.

4. The split between the advantaged fields, including the sciences, mathematics, engineering, medicine, and some of the social sciences, versus the disadvantaged fields, mostly the humanities and the arts and architecture, has grown. Faculty members in the latter areas get little or no federal support and few special awards for merit, and nobody consults with them. Some faculty members in these fields are embittered. The distinctions between being one of the "haves" and one of the "have nots" are more marked than ever before in American university history. This is even more so in 1994 than in 1963, when I spoke of "scientists affluent; humanists militant." The humanists have, however, benefited from the reduced teaching loads inaugurated by the scientists.

There have also been some repercussions that were not so clear in 1963 (or at least not so clear to me):

1. Other institutions, identified in the Carnegie Classification system as "doctoral granting" and "comprehensive" and even some of those as "liberal arts," have followed, but to a lesser degree, patterns set by the research universities. And the struggle

among institutions to enter the preferred category of "research universities" has intensified.

2. Applying for—only about one in three or four applications are actually granted—and managing and reporting on grants have taken more of the attention of many faculty members. Faculty members engaged in this "rat race" develop obligations to staff members and to graduate students that tie them to continued grant-seeking activity. (Obligations to staff drawn from minority groups can be particularly strongly felt and declining possibilities hard to handle.) Faculty members are now even more likely to be active leaders of teams. Managerial activity is one argument for lighter teaching loads and for greater reliance on teaching assistants. This activity often takes at least as much time as is freed up by lighter teaching loads. It should be noted, however, that teaching loads have gone down almost equally in non-rat-race areas, for example, rare and ancient languages.

3. Federal grant funds procured by individual faculty members have become a more important criterion, particularly in the less elite institutions, in academic promotions—to the detriment of the consideration given to teaching and to other internal service contributions.

4. Younger faculty members become desperate to get into the stream of grants; and some older faculty members, in contrast, obtain "tenure" within the granting system. The saddest cases are mid-life faculty members who entirely lose their extramural support.

5. Short-term projects take precedence over long-term projects in the course of the short-term funding and promotion cycles.

6. Faculty compensation has become more unequal. Some in the federal grant system, with pay for summer work and vacation periods, can add one-third or more to their basic annual income.

7. Shifts in federal policy have a greater effect on the destinies of individual universities. The recent shift to more polytechnic applied research has greatly advantaged such institutions as Georgia Tech, Virginia Tech, Texas A&M, UC-Davis, Penn State, and SUNY-Buffalo. These six averaged an increase in federal R&D of 101 percent from 1985 to 1992. Harvard, Stanford, MIT, and Berkeley averaged 62 percent.

8. Some individual universities become too dependent on a rising flow of overhead payments to finance their operations, and thus press too hard to expand areas that will increase that flow and to contract others that do not.

Federal research grants have come to have at least as important an impact on American universities in the twentieth century as the federal land grants had in the nineteenth; and both the service and the research functions have gained greatly as a result of these two federal initiatives. The common law marriages of the universities and the federal government have been uncommonly productive.

The Future of the City of Intellect

The original lecture on this topic was about how universities are among the most stable of all institutions (along with established religious institutions, out of which the universities, in part, developed in the Western and Muslim worlds) in their mechanisms of governance, in their basic beliefs, in their informal internal conduct. Yet today they are heavily buffeted by changes going on in the societies around them. And they come to be ever more central to those societies as advancing knowledge plays a more crucial role in economic development.

One of the frequent criticisms of the original lectures was that I analyzed the university that existed (albeit too ruthlessly) but that I had no vision of what it should be. In that third lecture, however, I certainly had a vision that both placed the university at the center of the universe and called for it, once again, to become more of a community of people and of interacting intellectuals across the fields of knowledge. I now realize, more than I did then, that this vision was really two visions, and that they are not inherently fully compatible. The former implied larger size and more specialization, and the latter smaller size and more commonality of interests—the best of Berkeley and the best of Swarthmore; but I would still hope that there may be ways to make them more compatible rather than less, although this may be only unguarded utopianism.

In 1963, I was generally optimistic about the workings of the knowledge process. Along with many university faculty members across the ages, I shared the view of Socrates that "there is only one good, knowledge, and one evil, ignorance." I shared the confident belief that the progress *of* knowledge leads to progress *through* knowledge.

In the 1990s I have more reservations, as do many others. Robert Heilbroner, a world-famous economist, has recently written that "the belief in progress . . . is today under such uneasy reappraisal"; and that the "idea of progress now stands at bay."[13] New knowledge, like addictive drugs, can have bad as well as good effects. And new knowledge has limits to its curative effects, as in directly controlling the population explosion or the eruption of ethnic and religious fundamentalism. Knowledge is not so clearly all good, and certainly not the one and only "one good." The university, consequently, needs to be more careful in what it does and less arrogant about what it claims it can do. So many of us should have realized all of this more fully so much earlier. We were too euphoric.

In 1963, I also identified some important changes taking place or about to take place in "the city of intellect" in terms of more specific "visions," including:

> The rise of the new biology and of interest in the creative arts
>
> The advance of community colleges as central institutions in a new era of universal access
>
> The "urgent issue of how to preserve a margin for excellence in a populist society"
>
> The acceptance of the American model of the multiversity as a "model for universities in other parts of the world"
>
> The failure of communism, in part, because it could not make as good use "of intellect in all intellects' many dimensions" as did the middle-class democracies

In the area of specific hopes for the future, however, my expectations were much too sanguine:

> That liberal knowledge would be (as well as should be) more central in the education of undergraduates—there has been much rhetoric but little action
>
> That many scholars might (and should) become more interested in more generalized views of society—instead, there is mostly fiercer specialization, not "a more unified intellectual world"
>
> That the university would give more attention to the development of its "brain" (its vision of what it best should and could do) as well as its "body" (its activities)—the body at least is still alive and mostly still well

I continue to hope for the early and full realization of all of these, but I no longer expect it.

Overall, I am somewhat less optimistic about the course of development of the university and its capacity for conscious self-improvement, just as I am somewhat less optimistic about the beneficent roles of knowledge. In the Preface to the 1982 edition, I sounded a warning, however, which I now repeat: beware of excessive swings of mood—from too much optimism in good years to too much pessimism in bad years.

I wrote that a decade before, after the student revolts of the 1960s and early 1970s, there were urgent questions about whether higher education could possibly recover. I noted that: many answers, in an orgy of hate and despair, were then being given— mostly that higher education generally and the university specifically were fated to decline. In the fall of 1973 I spoke at the annual meeting of the American Council on Education on "the moods of academia."[14] I noted some of the recently published books that stared out at me from my shelves with titles or subtitles such as these:

Academia in Anarchy (1970)
Academics in Retreat (1971)
Academy in Turmoil (1971)
American Universities in Crisis (1968)
Anarchy in the Groves of Academe (1970)

Back to the Middle Ages (1969)
Bankruptcy of Academic Policy (1972)
Blind Man on a Freeway (1971)
Blow It Up (1971)

Chaos in Our Colleges (1963)
Confrontation and Counter-Attack (1971)

Death of the American University (1973)
Degradation of the American Dogma (1971)
Destruction of a College President (1972)
Down and Out in Academia (1972)

Embattled University (1970)
Exploding University (1971)

Fall of the American University (1972)

This was only a sample, and the list could have been continued down through the alphabet. I said that "this is what some of our 'best' and our 'brightest' in higher education—defined as those who get books published—think of us." It still seems strange to me that persons with such highly trained intellects should also be such chameleons of mood when their own interests seem threatened—more reactive to current events than reflective of historical perspective.

But were these views correct? I answered: "To those who see only gloom and doom, we can say that much that is good is occurring. To those who say that everything fails, we can say that much is, in fact, succeeding. To those who see only problems, we can say there are possibilities available for their alleviation." I was speaking then as Chairman of the Carnegie Commission on Higher Education, engaged in what became a twelve-year survey of and recommendations about American higher education. The subsequent Carnegie Council on Policy Studies in Higher Education, which I also chaired, concluded in its final report in 1980 that, actually, in retrospect, "the 1970s . . . was a good decade for higher education."[15] Seldom have the fears of some academics at the time and the realities of history in retrospect been so far apart.

What have we learned about the American university out of the 1970s, which started out with such despair but ended up as a "good decade," and out of the turbulent 1960s? Certainly we have learned to treat with caution the overblown rhetoric and defective current judgments of many of our scholars studying higher education when they are under stress. Too many were themselves blind men on a freeway, not knowing which way the traffic was flowing.

This is a lesson that should not be rejected in 1994.

Notation

The idea of a "knowledge industry," it turns out, goes back a long way—at least to 1892 and Thomas Huxley: "The medieval university looked backwards; it professed to be a storehouse of old knowledge. . . . The modern university looks forward, and is a factory of new knowledge." I note, however, that I never used the phrase "knowledge factory" to describe the research university and that I find it abhorrent—unlike Huxley.[16] In fact, my description of the research university was quite different from that of a factory.

Reflections after the Revolts of the 1960s

Nineteen sixty-three was the worst possible time to have given the Godkin Lectures. They just preceded the student revolt at Berkeley in the fall of 1964, and, though at first read with understanding and approval by activist students then more interested in internal academic reform, the lectures were subsequently condemned when attention turned to more external issues where the university was viewed as part of a society they rejected. Also, the Berkeley faculty was then in a partial state of disenchantment. Berkeley was in the process of moving from being the one and only campus that really counted within the University of California to being one of several. It was sensitive to any criticisms of its obviously great achievements, and some faculty members thought I had singled out Berkeley for special criticism when, in fact, I was writing equally about Harvard and the other multiversities I had come to know quite well both in the United States and abroad (including, for example, the University of London). It was clearly not only at Berkeley that undergraduates were being neglected and that other developments I criticized were taking place, but to some faculty members at Berkeley it looked that way. Radical students and conservative faculty members were equally affronted by the idea of the "multiversity." And this was brought to my attention. Would I have chosen to give these lectures when I did knowing what I know now? The answer is absolutely "no."

The next question is whether I should have given these lectures as an active president regardless of the date, and the answer is "almost certainly not." Only one other sitting president in the twentieth century, to my knowledge, was as openly critical of the modern research university as I was, and that was Robert Maynard Hutchins. We shared some (but by no means all) of the same reasons, and he paid for his criticism. He was the more critical (with the University of Chicago as a partial exception, as what he called "the best there is") and the more acerbic and eloquent in his comments. He attempted to do far more about his criticisms, and he also paid the more for it. The almost universal presidential pattern is to speak in laudatory platitudes, and never to be indiscreet—better to be "pompous." This is not only what is routinely offered but also what is confidently expected and placidly accepted. I have concluded that it is a disservice to the presidency to speak otherwise; that it is not wise to be as frank and open as Bob Hutchins and I were; that discretion is the better part of valor—a rule that most presidents do not have to be told to obey.

Finally, should I have given the lectures ever? Here I conclude that they may have been helpful to some in advancing their understanding. Since I could not have written the lectures without first-hand experience, I should have waited until a few years after I left the presidency—but at that point it is unlikely that I would have been invited to give the Godkin Lectures at Harvard.

Postscript 1972 (Chapter 4), written for the second edition, followed the searing experiences of the 1960s. I tried to spell out better what I meant by the term "multiversity" and by the role of the "mediator." I am not sure, however, that had I done this earlier it would have led to a better reception of the lectures by their critics who would not have liked them anyway. I also reaffirmed some major themes of the original lectures as I do here once again. In 1972 I displayed, also once more, my overly optimistic hopes for the future. In 1972, these hopes included that some new presidential "giants" would come along to give leadership, even though I had earlier shown that such leadership was significantly harder to give under the new circumstances surrounding the presidency. What I referred to in 1972 as the unwritten Chapter 4 was later written in extended form in some of the reports of the Carnegie Commission and Council, which I came to chair.[17]

Attempted Reforms That Failed

Postscript 1982 (Chapter 5) looked back on the many intended internal reform efforts, particularly academic,[18] of the 1960s and 1970s which mostly failed, and then attempted to explain why. Externally originated efforts or pressures to change were more generally successful; and, again, why?

I was clearly wrong about one internal reform: the development of African-American Studies, Hispanic Studies, Asian Studies, Native American Studies, and Women's Studies—if these are looked upon as internal rather than external reform efforts; actually they were both. These areas of study have taken off in recent years. One campus I know well has more than one hundred courses in these areas in its catalogue. I think this is because, once these areas were opened up, students chose them in substantial numbers (sometimes encouraged by requirements), and then budgets and faculty positions followed closely on student choices of courses. I did not anticipate this because such courses have few vocational or professional uses, and students had been generally moving in vocational and professional directions. The search for supportive academic and social environments has been much greater than I anticipated. Also, these developments had much external support.

Chapter 5 was more concerned with attempted internal academic reforms. It gave less attention to the central internal political thrust of the student movement of the 1960s, which was what Wolff called "all power to the faculty and students."[19] This effort had some contemporary impact on greater faculty interest in student viewpoints and even has some continuing impacts, but, as a revolutionary change, it was a complete failure. No department that I know of in an operating college or university is now run on this basis, let alone an entire institution; and all those efforts at "free universities," including the Free University of Berlin, failed. The concept had several flaws in practice:

1. It rejected the interests of the surrounding society and ignored the need for its support. It sought to be a "state within a state," but a state that was not viable on its own, particularly with the sole purpose of "sustained critique."[20]
2. It neglected the administrative aspects of governance (no president and no trustees), as well as the judicial.
3. In the area of legislation, to which it was devoted, it sought to disenfranchise large elements of the total constituency by favoring the activists participating in mass meetings; it put the emphasis on tactics of confrontation and "no compromise"; it ignored the differing interests of faculty and students (and within each group). I note that participatory democracy as demanded by "new left" students as central to their program was more attractive to faculty when it was targeted at the president and the trustees than when it was aimed at the academic senate and individual departments. The "new left" students made a terrible tactical mistake when they attacked instrumentalities of faculty governance. Faculty support quickly turned to opposition. This was one major reason "the movement" disappeared more quickly than it arose. Participatory democracy went "off limits."
4. In practice, it resulted more in stalemate than in progress. This was inevitable.

Additionally, in Chapter 5, I neglected to mention the great impact of the demise of *in loco parentis* rules of a Puritanical nature and of the rise of *in loco parentis* advice of a "Mother Earth" aspect *(Prometheus Bound)* in matters of physical and mental health and of academic and professional advancement. *In loco parentis* took a new form: "Behold me."

A NEW AGE?
FROM INCREASING FEDERAL
RICHES TO INCREASING
STATE POVERTY

The American research university has thus far experienced four ages (the fourth only beginning), with, of course, more to come:

1. *Origins: 1810–1870.* The German model became increasingly attractive, initially only to a small number of American faculty members and presidents, after the founding of the University of Berlin in 1809. The establishment of Johns Hopkins in 1876 was the clearest single triumph for the German model. This development was joined by the creation of the land grant model by federal action in 1862.

2. *Slow growth: 1870–1940.* Many universities, both private and public, devoted more and more attention to research, although the primary interest, in terms of faculty time, remained teaching. Vannevar Bush, in his *Science: The Endless Frontier* (1945), found in a survey of 125 institutions that in 1940 about 20 million current dollars from all sources was being spent by them on research and engineering, and that about $10 million,

or half of the total, was concentrated in 10 universities which, regrettably, he did not identify. These were the "primary" research universities of that time.

3. Rapid expansion and extension of activity: 1940–1990. The first great explosion came during World War II, with MIT, Chicago, and Berkeley leading the way. A hot military war, a cold military war, and then a subsequent international industrial war helped to transform the world of the American research university. By the early 1990s, about 125 institutions were identified as "research universities," according to the Carnegie Classification system. For them, research was the dominant single faculty activity. In 1963, I had spoken of 20 such universities which then expended about half of the federal R&D going to all universities and colleges. In 1990, it took 32 universities to account for one-half of federal support for "academic science."

I include the 1970s in the period of rapid expansion and extension because, though federal R&D funds had stabilized, they were being divided up among more institutions and student enrollment was still increasing. The 1980s saw a revival of increases in federal R&D expenditures by universities (particularly 1983–1988) as the United States mounted its final (and successful) military and scientific challenge to the USSR. Also in the 1980s, the widely predicted "demographic depression" failed to take place.

4. Constrained resources: 1990–2015, and perhaps beyond. The prospects for a continued golden flow of money, from state resources in particular, appear to be less assured. The first reaction on campus was to try to ignore (or deny) what was happening—a reaction still prevalent among many faculty members. A second has been for administrators to take band-aid actions. The third is still evolving, and it potentially involves both administrators and faculty. It will be pressured by the new tidal wave of students affecting many institutions directly and others indirectly by the competition for resources.

The original Godkin Lectures looked at Age 3 from the standpoint of 1963. This fourth edition looks at Age 4 from the standpoint of 1994—in each case, too early to know at all fully what was (or is) happening, but not too early to begin to speculate and to prepare responses.

Nineteen sixty-three was a good year for the United States. The postwar economy was at its highest. Politically the theme was the "new frontier." It was also a good time for the American research university, already taking its place in world leadership. Nineteen ninety-four is not so good a year, either for the United States or for the American research university. But that does not mean that all is lost and gone forever. Moods can swing more than reality fully warrants. And nostalgic memories can be too rosy, including of Swarthmore in 1932, Berkeley in 1939, or Harvard in 1963.

Signs of Possible Internal Transformations and Rising Tensions

The status of the American research university is clearly less exalted than it was during its Golden Age. Internally, some of the conditions that I spoke of in the original Godkin Lectures have worsened, including some additional loss of attention to undergraduate students, and the additional loss of a sense of campus community by the faculty. As to the former, there may come to be something of a reversal as rising tuitions may help to offset falling concerns and failed consciences as undergraduates become more of a source of needed revenues. However, I am now more concerned than ever with the latter, since it is showing itself more and more in a decreased willingness of some faculty members to participate effectively in the duties of shared governance. All over the United States, presidents and provosts have acknowledged this trend in conversations I have had with them. It is also the observation of Henry Rosovsky of Harvard: "When it concerns our more important obligations—faculty citizenship—neither rule nor custom is any longer compelling . . . It is my distinct impression—'firm belief' would perhaps be a better expression—that there has been a secular decline of professorial civic virtue in FAS [Faculty of Arts and Sciences]."[1]

There are other rising concerns over the internal life of the campus. One is how effectively both diversity and excellence in faculty appointments can be assured during the interim period while more adequate pools of well-trained talent are created across-the-board.[2] A second is whether diversity leads in the direction of greater social integration or rather from the once externally enforced segregation toward more self-chosen internal separatism on the campus, and toward the teaching more of competitive and even antagonistic cultures than of an understanding of comparative cultures.

A third concern is the attack on rationality by a few scholars, particularly in the humanities, where the older "Western rationalistic tradition" in pursuit of contingent truth[3] (always still potentially subject to "falsification") is now being challenged, in an anti-positivistic assault, by the newer and more confident pursuit of absolute "beliefs" in the course of which "truth is made" instead of being "discovered"—more assertions and less verification. And a fourth concern, related to the third, is the extent to which the pursuit of "passions" and beliefs may replace (or heighten) the pursuit of "interests" in dividing up resources in the search for "truth" inside the university.[4]

Once (more than a century ago) it was the old religion and adherence to the faith that was being challenged by the new science and by meritocracy. Now it is "the Western intellectual tradition" that is being challenged by proportionality and by new humanistic revelations. This new set of challenges is convulsing some segments of the intellectual world and making it more difficult to handle internal polycentric conflicts. New quasi-religions now confront the old science.

Two additional long-term trends that seem to be taking place may be subject to faster evolution in a period of constrained resources accompanied by more external criticisms and attacks on current practices. If so, they may add to the tensions. The two trends I note are the changing status of the academic guild and, related to it, the changing forms of academic contracting.

The Academic Guild in Evolution. The professoriate is one of the remaining guild-like groups in American society, but this social configuration appears to be in the process of slow disintegration. A guild is marked by several characteristics, including sole control over entry, full internal self-governance, unwritten and informally enforced rules that seek to govern individual behavior, and life tenure of status via control over exit.[5] Each of these characteristics is undergoing some change. Some of it is inevitable for evolutionary reasons, some necessary for social reasons, and some desirable for ethical reasons. For example, control over entry via granting the Ph.D. and awarding tenure is more subject to surveillance, as in "affirmative action," self-governance to reduced participation by some members of the guild, communal rules of behavior to greater resort to self-chosen conduct, and tenure to externally imposed prohibitions, as in sexual or racial and ethnic harassment. Some of this erosion of guild-like status is coming from the outside in the form of influence over entry and continuance of tenure; and some from the inside, in the form of impaired commitment to self-governance and to understood codes of behavior.

When does a guild cease being a guild and what are the

consequences? Guild-like status goes back to Bologna and Salamanca and to Paris and Oxford and Cambridge. The professoriate now appears to be in the process of moving away from this historic status, and some of the adjustments may be traumatic. Eric Ashby, then vice chancellor of Cambridge University and the leading vice chancellor among the universities of the former British Commonwealth, once raised the question of whether or not the professoriate was a "disintegrating profession" that now needs "a Hippocratic Oath" and other reforms.[6] That question, as yet, has no definitive answer.

Changing Forms of Contracting. Human relations are mostly based on contracting of one form or another, and there are a multitude of forms. In the absence of contracting, pure anarchy (if there is such a thing), or at least chaos, results. Contracts take several generalized forms with infinite variations:

Explicit contracts. Precise and usually written.
Implicit contracts. Less precise and based on mutual understandings.
Incomplete contracts. Subject to intermittent interpretations and additions.
One-sided, open-ended contracts. One party or the other can make unilateral changes without constraints.

Academic contracting, as I see it, is undergoing fundamental changes. Traditionally, reliance has been placed on the implicit contract—on informal codes that are informally enforced, as in a "gentlemen's club" where some things are just not done. This system is breaking down in two different but related directions.

One direction is more assertion of the possibilities inherent in open-ended contracts, where faculty members or groups of faculty members can unilaterally determine changes in teaching loads, in time spent in non-university employment, in observance of office hours, in assent to participate in committee assignments, in willingness to consult and advise with colleagues, in use of institutional facilities for personal purposes. In this mode, though institutional obligations are being made more comprehensive, the open-ended nature of faculty obligations is being more actively explored.

In the other direction, and largely as a backlash, are greater institutional demands for more and more detailed designations of faculty obligations, with greater provision for administrative penalties and for independent judicial enforcement. Union contracts, in particular, are moving increasingly in this direction in institutions subject to collective bargaining. It may ultimately be management that insists on such bilateral contracts—just like society: more laws and more emphasis on systems of corrections.

This may all turn out to have been inevitable, although I like to think there may still be an element of conscious choice. My own observation is that organizations that confidently rely mostly on informal codes and implicit contracts are more effective and more satisfactory to their participants. The slow trend, however, seems to be in the direction of more standard industrial-type employment contracts.

Overall the campus may be in one of the earlier of the final stages of incorporation into society, of assimilation, of integration, of homogenization—no more "Ivory Tower," no more "Town and Gown."

Deterioration in Availability of External Resources

The biggest, newest, and most immediately pressing concerns lie, however, with the current and prospective external financial support for American higher education, including for research universities. These concerns over resources include the following:

1. In 1963, and during the whole period from the end of World War II to the early 1970s, productivity in the United States was rising at a rate of 3 percent per year. This rate dropped to

2 percent (the historical level since about 1860) and then more currently to 1 percent. At 3 percent, productivity (and the consequent potential standard of living) doubles in 25 years; at 2 percent, in 40; and at 1 percent, in 75. The availability of new resources for meeting national needs has gone down drastically. Productivity, it should be noted, is a very slippery subject. We do not measure it well (for some activities it is "unmeasurable"), and what we do measure we do not fully understand.[7] Consequently, predictions are very hazardous. They are hazardous, too, because the major component of sources of productivity increases, "advances in knowledge," is inherently unpredictable. It seems likely, however, that, if anything, current measures of productivity changes may underestimate actual increases, particularly because they do not fully take into account improvements in quality of products and services. On the other hand and ominously, the productivity of R&D expenditures in terms of new patents has been decreasing drastically. As Paul Krugman has written, "Productivity isn't everything, but in the long run it is almost everything."[8] In any event, we can no longer count on the assumption of the 1950s and 1960s that "abundance was here to stay."[9]

2. The revolt against taxes has put a ceiling, within total resources, on revenues available for public redistribution.

3. Total demands for public purposes have risen and continue to rise: for care of the aged, care of children and youth, health care at all ages, care of the environment. The national physical infrastructure has deteriorated and requires repair. The cost for prisons has gone up rapidly—from 4 to 8 percent of the state general fund in California over the past ten years, while higher education decreased from 13 to 9 percent. (For the nation as a whole, state expenditures for corrections have gone up 40 percent, whereas expenditures for higher education have decreased by 4 percent.) There is rising warfare within the welfare state—a

Table 3   Change in state appropriations for public colleges and
universities, 1991–92 to 1993–94 (adjusted for inflation)

State	Percent Change
California	−29
Montana	−15
Oregon	−12
Louisiana	−9
Vermont	−9
South Carolina	−8
Connecticut	−7
Kentucky	−7
North Dakota	−7
Virginia	−7
Alaska	−6
Maine	−6
Oklahoma	−6
Michigan	−5
Wyoming	−5
Indiana	−4
Minnesota	−4
Nevada	−4
New York	−4
Pennsylvania	−4
Arizona	−3
Idaho	−3
Delaware	−2
Ohio	−2
Washington	−2
Maryland	−1
Nebraska	−1
West Virginia	−1
Illinois	0
Kansas	0
Missouri	0
Rhode Island	0
Colorado	+1
New Hampshire	+1
New Jersey	+1
Arkansas	+2

State	Percent Change
Wisconsin	+2
Alabama	+3
Florida	+3
Hawaii	+3
Iowa	+5
Utah	+5
New Mexico	+6
North Carolina	+6
South Dakota	+6
Texas	+7
Mississippi	+10
Georgia	+12
Tennessee	+12
Total U.S.	−4

Massachusetts figures are not comparable with previous data due to changes in tuition policies.
Source: *Chronicle of Higher Education*, vol. 40, no. 10 (October 27, 1993), p. A29. Based on data compiled by Edward R. Hines and Gwen B. Pruyne of Illinois State University.

massive battle over the distribution and redistribution of scarce resources. A former director of finance for the state of California calls it a "war of knives," and observes that "higher education has no knife."

4. The nation went through a prolonged recession over the past several years which had the effect of weakening higher education and also creating each year a lower statistical base for future financing of public higher education.

As a consequence of the above, state funds for public higher education have fallen significantly overall (and for many different reasons individually among the fifty states; see Table 3.) State funds for higher education have fallen in recent years even when

Gross Domestic Product

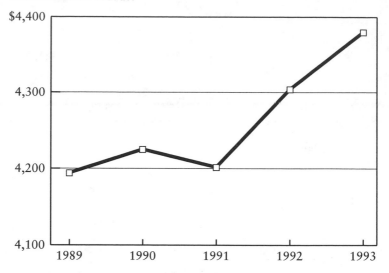

Figure 1   Gross Domestic Product, 1989–1993 (in billions of
constant 1982–1984 dollars). Data source: *Survey of
Current Business,* various years.

Appropriations

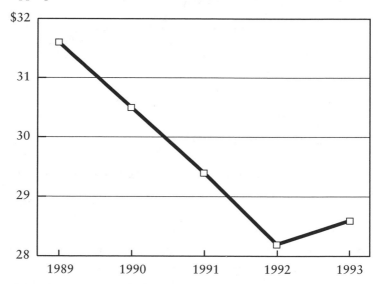

Figure 2   State appropriations for higher education, 1989–1993
(in billions of constant 1982–1984 dollars). Data source:
Grapevine, no. 392 (November–December 1993), Table 1
(Center for Higher Education, Illinois State University).

total gross domestic product has risen (see Figures 1 and 2 and Table 4). State expenditures for higher education are being placed, increasingly, in a "discretionary" category.

Shortly, Tidal Wave II of students will hit (1997) and continue to about 2015. This wave of additional students may be about one-third the absolute size of Tidal Wave I after World War II but will amount to much less of a proportionate increase—about 20 percent instead of 200 percent. It will, in any event, be substantial, perhaps three million students across the nation, and lead to an increase in some states by as much as 50 percent. In other states there will be no increases and there may even be reductions. Tidal Wave II, as Tidal Wave I, will directly impact community colleges and comprehensive colleges and universities more than research universities, but state (and federal) support of student enrollment at the former will be more competitive indirectly with overall financial support for the latter.

Federal funds for university research have slowed in their rates of increase generally over the period since 1953–1958 (see Figure 3 and Table 5). Prospects for the future are uncertain. The Cold War as the unassailable argument for support is over. "Commer-

Table 4   Changes in Gross Domestic Product and in state appropriations for higher education, 1990–1993 (constant 1982–1984 dollars)

Year	Percent change, GDP	Percent change in state appropriations for higher education
1990	0.7	−3.5
1991	−0.55	−3.6
1992	2.4	−4.1
1993	1.8	1.4

Sources for state appropriations: *Grapevine*, no. 392, November–December 1993. Normal, IL: Center for Higher Education, Illinois State University.

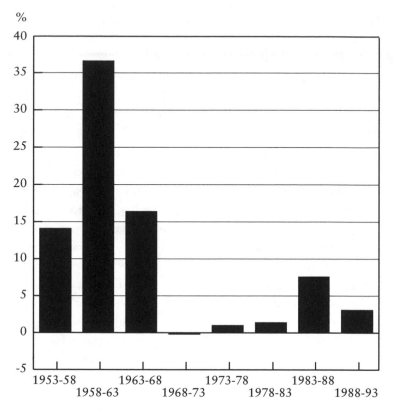

Figure 3   Percentage change (in constant dollars) in federal funds
for research and development at universities and colleges
(not including federal laboratories), 1953–1993, by
five-year intervals. Data source: Table 5.

Table 5   Annual change in federal funds for research and
             development at universities and colleges, averaged over
             5-year periods, 1953–1993

Years	Percent change
1953–1958	14.1
1958–1963	36.6
1963–1968	16.4
1968–1973	−0.2
1973–1978	1.0
1978–1983	1.4
1983–1988	7.6
1988–1993	3.1

For constant dollar amount, see p. 142.
Source: Calculated from U.S. National Science Board, *Science Indicators 1993* (Washington, D.C., 1994), Appendix Table 4-3, "U.S. R&D by Performing Sector and Source of Funds."

cial relevance," however, will continue to become more important.[10] In particular, how may federal and state support of Tidal Wave II students compete with support for research? How will the rising numbers of faculty members needed to keep up with the student numbers affect per-faculty federal R&D funds available?

It might be said that Multiversity I (federal riches at the national level) has given way to Multiversity II (poverty at the state level). Multiversity II, as a consequence, is being faced with enhanced guerilla warfare over resources—overall among competitors within the welfare state and, more specifically, within campuses, among campuses, between systems, and between public and private campuses for competitive advancement. In the latter context, the privates are generally favored since they are less dependent on state appropriations, but they are also threatened with the publics entering more actively into competitive private fund-raising. Multiversity II lives in a more Hobbesian world "of every man against every man."

Four Possible Confrontations in the University World of the Near Future—1997 to 2015

What may the consequences be:

1. *If* there is no substantial and continuing rise in the rate of productivity increases,
2. *If* the revolt against tax increases endures,
3. *If* the competitive demands for augmentations in public expenditures continue to rise among the many powerful claimants within the welfare state broadly defined to include education and public security, and
4. *If* Tidal Wave II of new students does not vanish? The potential additional students are already mostly born. It is uncertain, however, what will happen to the differential income resulting from college attendance, which rose enough in the 1980s to more than offset the expected "demographic depression," just as it had dropped enough in the 1970s to give rise to the announcement of the arrival of "the overeducated American." Also, it is uncertain what impacts rising levels of tuition may have on college attendance, and these impacts may be substantial, particularly at the community college level, but less so at the research university level.

How one evaluates each of these four "ifs" will determine expected prospects for the future, and evaluations will differ. My own evaluations are that there are inherent negative implications for higher education in each of these four areas, and that they reinforce one another. If so, there will certainly be severe consequences for the research universities and for all of American higher education.

I shall, in what follows, comment more specifically on the impacts on state-financed research universities.

CONFRONTATION ONE: THE PROFESSORIATE FACES A
SCARCITY OF RESOURCES

The American research university, along with all of American
higher education, has been blessed with rising resources and
expenditures on a per-student basis for a substantial period of
time (see Figure 4 and Table 6). (Note that this rise of expenditures is even more spectacular because many more of the students
are now at the lower-cost community college level.) These additional resources have made possible enormous improvements in
libraries, vastly greater facilities for advising students about their

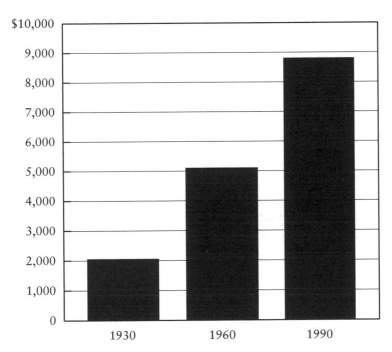

Figure 4   The rising tide of expenditures (educational and general)
per estimated full-time equivalent student in U.S. higher
education (in constant 1982–1984 dollars). Data source:
Table 6.

Table 6   Expenditures (educational and general) per estimated
full-time equivalent student, 1930–1990 (constant
1982–1984 dollars)

Year	Expenditure
1930[a]	$2,050
1960[b]	5,100
1990[c]	8,800

a. 1930 FTE enrollment assumed to be the same as head-count enrollment.

b. 1960 enrollment calculated as 83 percent of head count based on actual data that show 1970 as 79 percent.

c. 1990 is based on actual FTE enrollment.

Source: U.S. Office of Education; U.S. Department of Education; *Digest of Education Statistics,* various years.

careers, their health, and their academic possibilities, a spectacular augmentation of specialized courses (of greater benefit to faculty members than to undergraduate students), and in rising real salaries for faculty members even without a rise in their own measurable productivity. Affluence has advanced in higher education along with the rest of middle-income America. As a consequence, the professoriate has not had to be highly conscious of resource constraints. And efficiency has not generally been ranked among the highest of values in the academic world.

The professoriate is not well organized to consider issues of efficient use of resources. Many decisions with heavy cost consequences, including faculty teaching loads and size of classes, are made at levels far removed from direct contact with the necessity to secure resources. Departments usually operate on the basis of consensus, and it is difficult to get a consensus to cut costs. And among departments, the rule is senatorial courtesy—not to interfere with the conduct of others, however inadequate it may be.

Tenure is rated highly, not only the tenure of individual faculty members but also the tenure of departments and institutes once established—as several efforts at reduction of departments and institutes have dramatically shown in recent times. A threat to one is a threat to all. All this in an enterprise that is marked by an unusually high proportion of expenditures on personnel.

The call for effectiveness in the use of resources will be perceived by many inside the university world as the best current definition of evil.

Confrontation Two: Professorial Interests and Public Interests

The professoriate, quite naturally, is most interested in teaching loads, in real salary levels, in adequacy of resources for teaching and research, and in quality generally. The public, also quite naturally, is most concerned with assured access for students and low costs. Many states will be faced with the hard choices between maintaining access versus supporting research—and access likely will have the greater popular support; and between quantity and quality—and political pressures will lie more on the side of the former.

Confrontation Three: Presidential Duty and Presidential Survival

Presidential duty calls for matching, over the foreseeable future, expenditures with resources, while preserving access for students, quality in teaching and research, and institutional autonomy from excessive state interference; for concentration on the long run and overall welfare of the institution. Presidential survival depends, on the contrary, on not calling undue attention to longer-run difficult prospects, on making adjustments year by year, on choosing adjustments that lead to the least powerful immediate protests (as by cutting plant maintenance and the purchase of books), on encouraging early retirements on favorable terms, on postponing new appointments, and on not making adjustments that can be pushed up the line to trustees—or out to external authorities, or down to the provosts and deans, or that can be saved for the attention of successors. Survival depends heavily on not disturbing any current faculty members. Some presidents are dedicated more to duty and some more to survival—thus far in quite unequal proportions, in part because the latter at least survive. The positive contributions of the former, however, will appear the greater ten or twenty years later— mostly when such presidents are in early retirement. The reduction in the influence of presidents (and of trustees) over the years will often make survival seem to be the only realistic choice: "What can I do, anyway?"

CONFRONTATION FOUR: OVER-DEFINITION OF THE SOUL OF THE UNIVERSITY

One common definition (and my own) of what is most important is: high concern for student access, for faculty quality, and for institutional autonomy. The main alternative is a gradually diminished status quo in each area—and overall of the soul of the university.

It would be a much better world for the research university if resources were flowing in profusion, if there were no tight lid on public expenditures, if higher education were in a better position to compete for public funds, if the young people who constitute Tidal Wave II had never been born. But these are not the conditions of current reality. It is a time of testing by a new combination of problems and how to confront them. Some institutions and presidents will confront their problems actively, seeking to fight their way through to satisfactory solutions. They will do so out of institutional pride and confidence, out of the personal instincts of some of their leaders to meet challenges head on, out of availability of good high-level decision-making instrumentalities, and out of other personal and organizational resources. Some other institutions and presidents will confront their problems, take a careful look, and then turn tail and run.

The quality and character of leaders will be more important than in less troublesome times, as will the nature of the institution—the more favored private over the less favored public, the more favored applied polytechnic over the less favored "pure" and "basic" in terms of research orientation, and those in more prosperous versus those in less prosperous states (see Table 1). Thus: How led? How constituted? Where located? However led, however constituted, and wherever located, the research university, as all of American higher education, cannot escape the imperative of more effective use of resources—no more than can the health care industry.

Complicating the situation is the fact that there are more "free agents" among faculty members now than in past times, and the exercise of "free agency" under the prospective conditions will place less favored institutions under special hazard while the more favored will be even more greatly advantaged.

8

HARD CHOICES

Research universities, as well as all of American higher education, face some "hard choices"[1] which they are ill equipped to make. The response so far has been mostly the "politics of caution,"[2] and no presidential "giants" have as yet emerged to take leadership; indeed, it is problematical how many will. Those who do will be engaged in protecting the academic core against the periphery and the excellent versus the mediocre, in encouraging better use of high schools and extension programs and the new technology to replace on-campus classroom instruction at the lower levels of competency, in making selective academic decisions on merit rather than across-the-board political adjustments, in maintaining libraries and physical facilities from slow decay, in looking at long-term academic welfare rather than year-to-year political survival. In the course of this series of developments, and one way or another, some of the "multi" will be taken out of the "multiversity," which in the age of affluence too often took on too many peripheral activities of low quality.

Some research universities already are choosing the long-term academic-quality route, and among those I know best in California are Stanford, Berkeley, and UCLA. It is this capacity to take the hard road that has given them leadership in the past and will make more possible its continuation in the future. These institutions are facing the questions of what is most important to preserve at the highest levels of quality, and of what are the activities most worth doing. They are proving that they have "a brain" as well as "a body." Some other universities are engaged, instead, in making their Faustian bargains—the temptations of current indulgences are so very great. They leave the toughest decisions to the future and to external authority, and lose both quality and autonomy in the process.

Some universities will seize the opportunity to rebuild a more integrated community of scholars as they participate in rigorous consultations and make hard decisions about what they most want to be, about how they can improve teaching *and* research *and* the quality of citizenship *and* ethical conduct more generally within the confines of more constrained resources. Some universities have never lost their sense of an integrated intellectual community of scholars, and I note here as illustrations Princeton, Chicago, and Cal Tech. Each has been advantaged by smaller size; and each by living in an external physical community with its own identity. Princeton and Cal Tech also have greatly restricted their expansions of effort. Chicago, in particular, has a tradition of conversations across the boundaries of the several disciplines. Among the larger institutions, I have always marveled at the cohesion of Harvard, Stanford, Cornell, Yale, MIT, Brown, Berkeley, and Michigan, and I have wondered what the secrets of social alchemy are that give them each their special characters. I wonder, too, about Indiana, Chapel Hill, Madison, and Virginia, among others of the 125 or so research universities—despite their size and the heterogeneity of their activities.

All is not yet lost. The maintenance of federal R&D funds at current levels would still support an enormous research enterprise far beyond anything even dreamed about in that golden age of 1963, and it would still be the envy of the world. Mere maintenance of current levels of federal R&D, however, will be particularly hard on the many current younger scholars trying to get established, and it will make no provisions for the new faculty members needed to accommodate additional students.

The bigger problem for all of higher education, from which the research university is, however, substantially shielded (most fortunately), will be to accommodate the vast additional numbers of students. Pressures will be placed on faculty teaching loads, on class sizes, on use of teaching assistants, on maintaining existing admissions standards. There will be many "hard choices," and they will be faced mostly at the presidential level, at a time when the presidency is, generally, in a weakened position. The most difficult period of "hard choices" in accommodating students, however, will be over by about 2015. The University of California in its entirety is in an especially difficult situation because the Master Plan of 1960 called for it to accommodate the "top" 12.5 percent of high school graduates (with "top" subject to changing definitions). It will thus be even more than usually difficult for it to adjust by raising admissions standards. Campuses within the system that have reached their targeted growth, however, are potentially protected from enrollment pressures by expansion on other campuses. For most public institutions of higher education, to one degree or another, the difficulties inherent in the new context will intensify substantially, beginning with the fateful year 1997.

Private universities and colleges, in the meantime, will hardly be affected by mass student pressures, and they will generally be in a comparatively advantaged position. They have two additional advantages: (1) greatly lowered taxes on the very wealthy, who are sharing this largesse through their gifts to private university fund-raising campaigns at levels never before experienced; and (2) greatly increased income to the well-to-do and wealthy as a result of income redistribution that has advantaged them over those with moderate and low incomes during the past twenty years, enabling them better to afford higher tuitions. Attached more to the private economy which prospers in its higher reaches, the private colleges and universities generally have better prospects than the public, which are more attached to the suffering public economy. Some of these private institutions will live in a world apart, fully insulated. Also comparatively advantaged are those public universities that are viewed more as "private," as in Michigan and Texas, where there are no or few private competitors. Among the approximately 125 research universities in the United States, about 40 are private and 85 are public, and among the public, a few are "private-public." The private and private-public also have greater alumni pressure, as well as assistance, to maintain quality. Thus the future of research universities (and all of higher education) appears to be substantially bifurcated, with one fork (the private) generally pointing level or even up and the other generally down—there will be exceptions.

Directions of Responses in the Shorter Run (1990–2015)

Signs of the future are already emerging, particularly for the public research universities:

1. *More privatization.* Greater reliance on tuition. The Carnegie Commission once suggested, based on relating costs to benefits,[3] that a reasonable general rule might be that students bear the burden of one-third of educational and general costs, with spe-

cial attention being given to differential tuitions in areas that lead to high-income professions.

More income from sales of services and from patents.

More cultivation of alumni.

More R&D funds from industry. (Industry funds for university R&D were 4 percent of federal in 1970 and 13 percent in 1993.)[4]

In the 1860s, there was the land grant university, in the 1960s what I called the "federal research grant university," and in the future may lie increasingly the "private grant" university.

2. *More federalization.* Adam Smith long ago set forth the three major areas for governmental responsibility as protection from external and internal violence, protection of individuals from injustice and oppression (which allows an opening to the welfare state), and provision of an infrastructure including basic education. The Great Depression added guidance of the economy to protect it against depression and then, later, inflation. Care of the environment has also been added in more recent times. Increasingly, particularly as the economy has been slowing down, government responsibility for economic growth has also been added. This latter assignment involves enhancement of labor skills and encouragement of research and development.[5]

In the United States, individual states are mostly in charge of providing basic skills (primary and secondary education) and advanced skills for local residents preparing for local and regional labor markets (community colleges and comprehensive colleges and universities). Industry is responsible for plant-specific skills and company-specific applied technology. The federal government, increasingly, is held accountable for higher skills for national and international labor markets, as in science and engineering and medicine, and for basic research as well as for the more generally useful forms of applied research (the research universities). The long-term trend is for the federal government to have more overall responsibility for high-level training and high-level research. Health care is the area now most completely federalized in research support and high-level skill development.

Responsibility for economic growth means, among many other things, the federal government's taking more responsibility for the overall welfare of the research university. As prospects for growth in income have become less assured, the public is more and more insistent that the federal government be held responsible for per capita economic progress. With increases in productivity based somewhere in the area of 40 percent on "advances in knowledge" and 20 percent on increases in skills, the federal government is forced to take more interest in education at all levels (as in "Goals 2000") but particularly in higher education and especially in the research university. The federal government could help additionally by giving more subsidies to graduate students in the fields most essential to productivity increases, by providing more funds for new research facilities and equipment, by increasing "overhead" allowances to match those given in industry, and by increasing funds for "academic science" roughly related to the increasing numbers of faculty members in "academic science" fields in research universities.

3. *More cultivation of general public support.* The land grant university was aimed at service to agriculture and industry. At one time, the College of Agriculture made contact with a majority of citizens in the state, and the borders of the campus really were the boundaries of the state. Many state universities, in more recent times, have concentrated mostly on the cultivation of governors and legislators, rather than on the public as a whole. This is no longer enough. Two areas now offer particular opportunities. One is education, where Schools of Education, instead of being specialized liberal arts colleges, might better emulate the old College of Agriculture and work with every school in the

state through extension services and experiment stations. The second is health, where, including through the Area Health Education Centers that the University of North Carolina developed so effectively under the presidency of William Friday, universities with medical centers can make contact with most hospitals and doctors and nurses in the state. A reinvigorated land grant model might yet save the German-model state research university.

4. *More attention to effective use of resources.* Charging "full cost" and providing unlimited across-the-board programs are no longer viable as the basic principles of operation. Costs could be more carefully scrutinized. And not all universities need to provide coverage of all fields of knowledge; rather, some might concentrate more on what is most needed and what they do the best. There is no clear proof that quality of instruction is precisely related to student/faculty ratios, nor need teaching loads be uniform across-the-board; rather, they should be related to the degree to which the individual field is engaged in creating and disseminating new knowledge. Research universities need not provide basic skills and remedial instruction, but rather might transfer this responsibility to high schools, to community colleges, to extension services, or to employment of electronic technology. Facilities can be more fully utilized on a year-round rather than a nine-month basis. Some students can be provided with a three-year degree opportunity. Effective use of resources, overall, can be improved at a significant level.

5. *More pluralistic leadership.* Each of the above requires more administrative effort by more people—to contact alumni, to service and persuade the public at large, to get better results from fewer resources, to work at the federal level, to make contact with each industry and each profession in areas of attention. This requires many more ambassadors, more publicists, and also more budgetary analysts for the sake of more careful use of

resources. This suggests greater decentralization of administrative responsibilities, which will better connect each operating unit with the fullness of reality ("every tub on its own bottom," as has traditionally been the case at Harvard—though this has some costs in allowing some fields potentially to fall below the generally very high levels, a problem Harvard is seeking to correct). This, in turn, suggests longer-term service by administrators down the line to make external contacts and to take responsibility for internal effectiveness, further suggesting more careful attention to the selection of presidents, deans, and department chairs. It also suggests more use of "provosts" at the level of schools and colleges to handle internal academic affairs. Presidents, then, would presumably concentrate more on the selection of deans and departmental chairs, and devote more attention to their coordination, guidance, and encouragement: more all-around pluralistic leadership. The emphasis will be more on team leadership, and that requires more attention to the creation of teams. Fred Balderston has called attention to these considerations: "balance in functional expertise," "high mutual confidence," and avoidance of "tendencies to split" the administration for the sake of the interests of functional constituencies.[6] This suggests that the president be able to build and maintain the team of his or her own choice.

6. *More attention to longer-term directions of movement.* I avoid the word "planning." First, because external conditions can change rapidly and there are so many uncertainties. Second, because it suggests there is such a thing as an "optimal" future for the institution. There are so many activities and so many constituencies that it is impossible to define maximum "welfare" with any precision. Third, I avoid the term because universities internally change so slowly. Faculty have tenure, and teaching and research units at least have seniority rights. The possible

changes in academic personnel and activities, except in periods of fast growth, are in a range normally somewhere below 5 percent a year—universities do not go out of business, or drop major activities because they are not currently profitable, or engage in major layoffs. To put it another way, only a small fraction of activities are in active competition for resources at any one moment.

It is possible, however, to have long-range goals to guide short-term incremental changes—a sense of what is more important and what is less. It is also possible to have good processes of consultation and decision-making to choose long-term directions of movement. These processes need to compensate for the fact that many presidents have a short-term horizon. This suggests substantial involvement by longer-term leadership within the trustees and faculty; but also longer terms for presidents so that there is less disparity between their horizons and those of their institutions—the Harvard customary twenty-year term.

A list of long-term directions might include:

Improve access on an equal opportunities basis
Concentrate on core fields
Keep faculty salaries competitive
Maintain libraries and physical plant
Preserve institutional autonomy by high quality of university conduct (nearly half the states have recently been investigating how to influence or even directly control faculty teaching loads)

7. *Consideration of protection for the "non-market" functions.* Higher education is becoming more market-oriented—the student market, the research market, the service market. But there should be more to a university than that. Specific actual markets do not express all the needs of society for university attention. Some such non-market needs are training for good citizenship, advancing cultural interests and capabilities of graduates, providing critiques of society (we hope from a scholarly

perspective), and supporting scholarship that has no early, if ever, monetary returns. There are social benefits of universities that go beyond what sells in the markets—thus the need to encourage "general purpose" support.

From Guarded Optimism to Guarded Pessimism to Guarded Optimism and Why

What about the longer run? This is mostly guesswork. Among other things, there are bound to be "wild cards" in the future as in the past—World War II was one such "card," as were the student revolts in the 1960s, the "demographic depression's" failure to develop in the 1980s, and the collapse of productivity increases since about 1970—unforeseen or largely unforeseen developments.

The *biggest uncertainty* we can now clearly recognize is what will happen to productivity in the economy. The most substantial negative force in this area is the rising share of "handicraft" employment, as in health care and education, which is now at about 75 percent of all employment, and the falling share of productivity-prone employment, as in agriculture and industry and communications, which is now at about 25 percent. The biggest potential positive force is further "advances in knowledge," perhaps particularly in the areas of usable energy, of new materials, and of biotechnology, in each of which advances might be almost limitless, and further exploitation of the possibilities of electronic technology. It would be very helpful to have another "transformational" development such as the railroads once were.

One thing, however, is almost certain, and that is that the research university, with its contributions to advances in knowledge and to higher skills, will become increasingly important to the maintenance of, and possible improvements in, society. It will continue to be one of the most necessary institutions in the nation. Frank Press has noted that the greatest advantage the United States has in world-wide competition is that we have "the largest and best trained force of scientists and engineers in the world. . . . This enables us more than anyone else to take advantage of emerging technologies and to harvest the wealth they create." And he raises the question of whether it is "adequate for what lies ahead" for support for science and technology to rise only "at about the same rate as the economy." Instead, we should "capitalize on our leading position in science and technology."[7] This means, I would add, that we should "capitalize" on our research universities. Productivity, it has been said, is not everything, but there is almost nothing else so important. A return to a 3 percent annual increase in productivity would be a magic cure for much of the current malaise affecting higher education.

A *second great uncertainty,* beyond what will happen to productivity, is whether the nation actually will take full advantage of one of its greatest assets. Fortunately, this is made more possible because of the small proportion that federal "academic science" support is of the total gross domestic product—less than two-tenths of 1 percent. Thus it can more easily be raised without impinging unduly on other uses of the GDP. But it remains open what priority will, in practice, be given to the research university by federal and state authorities. Note that federal funds for student aid, to a degree, compete with funds for academic science, and Tidal Wave II will greatly increase claims on federal aid for student access. Just as with the states, the federal government will face competing priorities within its support of higher education, as well as competition from claimants outside higher education. What will the priorities be?

As society goes, so goes the university; but, also, as the university goes, so goes society. The progress of knowledge remains so central to the progress of civilization. But there is no assured current prospect for another golden age for the research university in the foreseeable future.

A *third great uncertainty* is how the new resource constraints may mesh with the current signs of possible internal decay and rising tensions noted in Chapter 7. The internal life of the campus may never again be quite the same; the professorial form of employment so distinctive; the professoriate so autonomous. How effectively will the research university of the future conduct itself? At the moment, at least, the university world has hardly begun to try to take control of its future even within the confined limits of its potential influence.

If I were to add a *fourth uncertainty,* it would be whether or not the greatly improved hardware and software for the new electronic technology may, at last, start to penetrate teaching as it has already research and administration; whether the "Fourth Revolution,"[8] once so confidently expected, will finally take place. The experience to date suggests that each new technology adds to but does not totally supplant prior technology—oral teaching added to apprenticeship experience, the written word added to the spoken word, printing added to handwriting, and it seems likely that the "chip" will add to but not replace all the methods that have gone before.

I am now less assured about the future than I was in 1963. Then I noted the "generally optimistic tone" of the lectures. They were generally optimistic, but the optimism was a guarded one. I saw dangers ahead, but no great uncertainties about the fast-rising supremacy of the American research university. Thirty years later, I have questions:

1. What will happen to national productivity?
2. What priority will American society give to higher education in general, and the research university more specifically, in the distribution of available resources?

3. Will higher education, including the research university, take control of its future by responding in aggressive and wise ways?

I have "guarded pessimism" about the current period (1990–2015), and I have set forth the reasons for this in the above discussion. However, I return to "guarded optimism" about the long-term future because, after the problems of Tidal Wave II are past, I count primarily on the answer to question 2 above: that American society will give a high priority to higher education and to the research university within it. And secondarily on the answer to question 3: that our institutions of higher education will respond at least adequately to the new context.

I have moved from guarded optimism to guarded pessimism, but I remain an unguarded Utopian: I believe that we can become "a nation of educated people,"[9] and that our institutions of higher education will find better ways to associate "masters and scholars" together in learning communities, as well as better ways for masters to associate in their thinking across, and within, lines of fiercer specialization.

How may it all work out? We do not know. The research university is ever more essential to society. Yet higher education faces more competition for resources to finance its essential contributions. We need the research universities more but may be able to afford them less. This clash of prospects is the basic reality. Which way will this turn of history move the university: up or down? And what will be the roles of conscious choice and action?

The original Godkin Lectures ended with these words: "These are the uses of the university." They are still the uses of the university—better knowledge and higher skills, and they both become ever more important. It will be a sad situation if, over the long run, public investments in prisons continue to take a higher relative priority than investments in universities; and if, internally within the universities, preservation of the status quo takes priority over an aggressive commitment to access, to quality, and to autonomy. But higher education in the United States is built on three-and-one-half centuries of triumph, not tragedy. Past triumphs came in response to new opportunities and additional flows of resources, however, and a further triumph under current and prospective circumstances may well be less than fully assured. And, quite understandably, higher education is responding more slowly and more reluctantly to the current challenges. Nevertheless, the longer-run destiny is, I remain convinced, if not further triumph, at least a satisfactory series of responses.

There are some certainties: the university will continue to have its essential uses; the society, as I quoted Alfred North Whitehead in concluding those long-ago lectures, that "does not value trained intelligence is doomed"; and, I now add with caution, the university that does not fully dedicate itself above all else to the continuing advancement of trained intelligence is also doomed.

9

THE "CITY OF INTELLECT" IN A CENTURY FOR THE FOXES?[1]

In 1963 in the Godkin Lectures at Harvard, I referred to the American research university as a "City of Intellect"—a very busy place with a multiplicity of activities, many of them unrelated to one another, and I guessed at its future.[2] I chose the term, City of Intellect, to contrast the research university with the "village" of the liberal arts college composed of close friends and colleagues, and with the "one-industry" towns of the schools of agriculture and law and medicine, standing alone or grouped together in polytechnics with a single-minded devotion to one profession or industry.

The twentieth century was a grand century for the cities of intellect. The century, that golden century, is now past, never to be replicated. I welcome this opportunity to play, once again, the tantalizing guessing game about the future, although I realize it is a game at which one wins only under very special circumstances. My 1963 lectures came at a time of those special circumstances. Those lectures turned out to be very prescient. I am not convinced that their foresight can be duplicated in the year

2000, but trying to look ahead may have some value, such as helping to identify the types of leaders to choose and the problems they might encounter.

The 1963 lectures were partly celebratory. The "multiversity" was central to the further industrialization of the nation, to spectacular increases in productivity with affluence following, to the substantial extension of human life, and to worldwide military and scientific supremacy. In 1963 I wrote from an American point of view that "the wave of the future may more nearly be middle-class democracy, with all its freedoms, through its better use of intellect in all of intellect's many dimensions, than the 'dictatorship of the proletariat' . . ."[3] The late 1980s warrant changing that "may be" to "is." American leadership came to be based on our "better use of intellect," above all through the research university.

The situation in 1963.   But the 1963 lectures also identified the pathologies of the modern university and offered the first comprehensive list of its inherent diseases, some of them serious:

Rising federal influence over the direction of intellectual endeavors, most notably at that time still directed toward weapons of mass destruction.

Elevation of the sciences above the humanities and the social sciences, creating a widening gap between the "hard" and "soft" sides of intellectual life, and between the "rich" and the "not so rich" participants.

The valuing of research and service over teaching, with particular neglect of undergraduates, resulting in a reorientation of the campus from internal instructional to external service concerns—a crucial reorientation.

Creation of a new class of faculty entrepreneurs, chasing federal and philanthropic dollars, who replaced the secluded scholars

of yore. And the creation of a new type of administrator measured both by the money he or she is able to attract and by the
degree of his or her benign neglect of educational policy issues.
The president teaching moral philosophy gave way to the president with hat in hand.

At the same time came federal concentration on greater equality
of opportunity, and campuses doubled and tripled in size and
many new ones were started. Some observers spoke of the expanded campus as the "megacampus" analogous to the mega-
lopolis. The cities of intellect, among all of higher education,
were the most federalized.

My 1963 description of the new reality was revolting to many
in academe. David Riesman, in a review of my lectures, said I
had held up a mirror to the American professoriate and some
who did not like what was reflected tried to smash the mirror,
as did also some students.[4] But others held up mirrors that
reflected a similar picture. Both the triumphs and the pathologies
that were developing in 1963 are now seen by all.

How did I come to be among the first to explore this new
world? To begin with, I was asked to give some lectures and I
talked about what I knew. What I knew was a large and increasingly nationally competitive university that was eagerly responding to the billions of dollars of available federal research money,
including much for military research. When I had been a campus
chancellor within that university, I had kept open office hours
one afternoon a week for students to come in to see me. Many
came. I heard complaints from students who came to campus to
listen to Nobel laureates but who saw mostly teaching assistants—some of whom could not even speak English; complaints
of large classes and "true-false" exams; complaints of knowledge
split up into so many small pieces that a "liberal education"

could only be cobbled together with difficulty; complaints of too many in loco parentis rules—a torrent of complaints.

I gave those Godkin Lectures before a very sophisticated audience. I could not give the usual presidential oration about the glories of higher education and, in particular, of one's own institution. I thought I had to be more realistic and less celebratory than that. Henry May, professor of history at Berkeley, called the lectures the "least discreet" lectures ever written by an American university president.[5] I was telling the truth about American higher education as I then saw it, an indiscretion.

I wish that today, however, I might again be so prescient about the shape of things to come, but I cannot. First of all, I have long since left administrative involvement in a leading university. Also, I am no longer so in touch with student life. More importantly, however, I think having a clear view of the future is now much more difficult, perhaps impossible. We live in an age of too many discontinuities, too many variables, too many uncertainties, as almost any university president today can certify.

What I did in 1963 was to identify the three current greatest impacts on higher education in America and indicate their possible consequences. I was working with certainties, not making predictions. These impacts were obvious. One was the advent of universal access to higher education. The second resulted from the decision by the federal government at the beginning of World War II to base scientific research within the universities instead of building its own laboratories or relying on industry alone. The third was the enhanced availability of resources. The great challenge was to meld them all together as quickly and effectively as possible.

The commitment to universal access to higher education had begun with the land grant movement of the 1860s, opening access to the sons and daughters of farmers in an agricultural nation. It was given a big push forward by the GI Bill of Rights after World War II. Half of the students who utilized this program came from families from which no member had ever before gone to college. And the labor market was ready to absorb the graduates.

I became involved in creating the Master Plan of 1960 for Higher Education in California, which guaranteed that there would be a place in college for every high school graduate or person otherwise qualified who chose to attend. California was the first state to make such a commitment. Then, in the 1970s, the Carnegie Commission on Higher Education, which I chaired, concentrated on securing federal grant support for needy students to meet the costs of attendance and argued the merits of affirmative action.

Increasing demands for access led to the explosive growth of community colleges and the transformation of teachers' colleges into polytechnics. Enrollments in higher education tripled in the fifteen years between 1955 and 1970. American higher education had been a port of entry into the time-honored professions of theology, teaching, law, and medicine and into high-class social status. It now became a port of entry to the new economy, which placed a heightened priority on "human capital" in its many forms and on the middle class.

Higher education became even more of an adjunct to an immense and changing labor market. In the United States higher education has always been occupationally oriented; the original liberal arts colleges trained men to enter the ministry, teaching, and the practices of law and medicine. By the 1970s we were even advised to accept the advent of the "overeducated American," as described in Richard Freeman's famous book—overeducated for the needs of the labor force. Demand for educated persons was decreasing with the arrival of a series of recessions.

Supply was going up as the tidal wave of students of the 1960s graduated into the labor market and as more women entered it. The economic return to a college degree dropped precipitously. Then, in the 1980s, the feared "demographic depression" (that is, lower enrollments due to a smaller number of eighteen to twenty-four-year-olds in the population) never developed as the economic return to a college degree advanced to unheard-of levels. Many students came to college looking for job training, not a philosophy of life, as the Astin surveys demonstrated.[6] Enrollments in engineering, business administration, and computer science went up drastically, and the departments involved became among the most dominant on campus. College became less a professional and class-oriented institution for an elite and more a market-oriented instrumentality for the masses. It was a fundamental restructuring.

The second great impact came when the federal government decided to advance basic scientific research through the universities. There were alternatives, including government agencies, as in the Soviet Union and France, and private industrial enterprises, as in Japan. The crucial document for the postwar period was Vannevar Bush's 1945 report to the president, *Science, the Endless Frontier.*[7] The federal government was the suitor; faculty members in the research universities, the all too eager maidens. The teaching university of old was changing almost overnight into the research university. The approximate half dozen that existed by the end of World War II, in particular MIT, Chicago, and Berkeley, exploded into one hundred by the end of the century.

The teaching university metamorphosed into the "research university" in the sense that many in the faculty devoted their primary attention to their research and not to their teaching.[8] Teaching loads dropped by one-half or more from what they had been historically, not only in areas heavily funded by the federal government, but across the board. Teaching attention that was once devoted to undergraduates was increasingly directed toward graduate students. Campus-wide faculty committees on educational policy and on the curriculum withered away. Faculty member influence at the university came to parallel receipt of federal research funds. Physics and chemistry gained influence, and English literature lost. Leading research professors became world citizens.

Faculty members eagerly responded to the new markets. Wherever they could, they oriented themselves toward obtaining federal research dollars and industry consulting fees. Faculty salary scales, traditionally based, as in the case of teaching loads, on policies of "internal justice," now became more determined by alternative opportunities in external markets, causing much exaltation and much resentment, but also an improvement in faculty quality.

Administrators were more often drawn off campus, chasing resources for their greatly expanded enterprises. Institutions came to be ranked increasingly by their comparative "financial resources" per faculty member. Institutions once oriented toward religious morality, or self-chosen intellectual interests, or class status, were now increasingly market-oriented—Karl Marx's "cash nexus."

These two great developments, universal access for students and faculty conversion from teaching to research, have had many repercussions. In my 1963 lectures I made one big mistake: I foresaw student revolts but I misjudged their nature. I thought they would be based on student neglect by faculty due to concentration on research. This neglect was a background factor, but not the main orientation of activist students. Just as faculty members were turning their attention to federal contracts and to consulting fees off campus, students on their own were turning their attention to external interests, specifically to civil rights and the war in Vietnam. I did say that "a few of the 'nonconformists' have another kind of revolt in mind. They seek, instead, to turn the university, on the Latin American or Japanese models, into a fortress from which they can sally forth with impunity to make their attacks on society."[9] The vast expansion of student enrollment had turned what might otherwise have been small-scale attacks into massive assaults.

Along with these two enormous impacts on higher education came an unprecedented period of prosperity. Increases in productivity per hour of work rose to 3 percent a year, creating the possibility of doubling the per capita flow of goods and services cumulatively in a single generation, which resulted in rapid advances in affluence. It made possible a flow of resources that tripled the size of the higher education establishment and increased many times over support for university science. It also helped create good jobs for college graduates.

These three forces made possible the best, but still less than perfect, age of higher education in all American history and, in particular, the rise in eminence of the research university. Universal access, a greatly increased emphasis on scientific research, and high prosperity together lifted American higher education to the forefront of the new frontier and the new society where it has remained, although in diminished degree, for the rest of the century at the very center of human progress. And these three forces also brought American higher education to the forefront of higher education around the world.

The twentieth century was also a great liberating century for colonial populations, for populations under dictatorships around the world, for women, and for students. Old authorities crumbled or adapted both in society and on campus.

The new century. Now in the year 2000 we face the next tidal wave of enrollments, the grandchildren of the GIs. We also face a new and quite different century. Until about three hundred years ago, the future appeared absolutely certain—it was to be a replication of the past. Afterward the assurance of continuing material progress dominated the future. Now, at the start of the twenty-first century, this assurance of progress has given way for some, including me, to a sense of apprehension: we fear the nuclear bomb, environmental deterioration, the population explosion, the manipulation of DNA, the possibility of atomic and biological terrorism, and much else.[10] There is also apprehension about the future of higher education in America that affects all planning.

In the 1960s we were confident of progress in higher education. We made plans for twenty, thirty, forty years ahead, certain of their realization. Now the time horizon for planning is three or five or ten years. Who dares now to look forty years ahead with the same sense of assurance that we had in the University of California Growth Plan of 1960? How daring, how arrogant that would be! The plan of 1960 for the period to 2000, not so incidentally, was realized in many respects.[11]

There are, it appears to me, several reasons, beyond the general sense of apprehension, why it is harder today to develop an assured vision of the future and to make plans than it was in 1960:

> To begin with, I see no three forces so compatible, so dominating, and so welcomed at work as were universal access, assignment of the advancement of the "endless frontier" to the universities, and unprecedented prosperity. However, the new emphasis on research and the older emphasis on teaching were not as compatible as we first assumed; they turned out to be incompatible at the undergraduate but not the graduate level. The German

Humboldt model assumed that teaching is always and in all ways improved by engagement in research. It is not. Educational policy for undergraduates was neglected, and much teaching of undergraduates was turned over to teaching assistants.

Authority within the university is more circumscribed in making plans than ever before—more checks and balances by governments, by the courts, by faculty members, by students.

There is much more competition for public resources than in the 1960s, including for health care, primary and secondary education, and control of crime, so that more attention must be given to securing financial resources for higher education's operations, and less effort is available to plan for the future.

Perhaps above all, higher education is going through its first great technological change in five centuries—the electronic revolution. Late confrontation with fundamental technological change is the main reason why universities are the major institutions in the western world that have changed so little over the past five centuries. Agriculture, transportation, industry, and the military have all been impelled forward by new technology. Now it is higher education's turn. It is too early to tell in detail how the electronic revolution will affect higher education, but it is likely to be dramatic.[12]

There are more contradictory variables, more uncertainties, more checks and balances, more unwelcome developments. The only certainty is uncertainty.

Leadership for the twenty-first century: hedgehogs or foxes? This leads me to ask how we should approach the next century— as "hedgehogs" or as "foxes," referring to the famous essay by Isaiah Berlin.[13] "The fox knows many things, but the hedgehog knows one big thing"—or perhaps two or three. Hedgehogs "relate everything to a single central vision," to "a single, universal, organizing principle in terms of which alone all that they are and say has significance"; while foxes "pursue many ends, often unrelated and even contradictory," and they "lead lives, perform acts, and entertain ideas that are centrifugal rather than centripetal, their thought is scattered or diffused, moving on many levels, seizing upon the essence of a vast variety of experiences and objects" without fitting them into a "unitary inner vision." The hedgehog tends to "preach"—"passionate, almost obsessive"; while the fox is "cunning"—clever, even sly. Order versus chaos; unity versus multiplicity; the big vision versus adjusting to miscellaneous unanticipated events; certainty versus uncertainty.[14]

Isaiah Berlin was not a naturalist, nor am I, but I was a farm boy in eastern Pennsylvania and dealt with the equivalents of hedgehogs and foxes, and I thought both categories were engaged in the same frenetic search for bits of food and on the edge of starvation. I saw none thinking big or little thoughts or any at all except about food. However, I do agree with Berlin in the distinction between big vision situations and personalities and many small-item situations and personalities, and for this reason I shall continue to use the terminology of Berlin, although it offends my sense of naturalistic reality.

In the 1960s many of us had a hedgehog view of the three big forces at work: universal access, progress through science, and increasing productivity; and we were correct. But we also had blinders on and looked straight ahead. We too often ignored the pathologies. And we seldom saw the rise of the student rebellion until too late and then treated it too often as just an interference with the urgent pursuit of our visions. Academic leaders of this new century, or at least of its early decades, may be able to identify no great single vision to guide them or great and compatible forces to dominate them; they may need to look in more directions, to be sensitive to many diverse opportunities and to many threats. They may best be foxes or "entrepreneurs" in Bob Clark's terminology, looking around every bush, avoiding every trap, eating everything that happens to come along that can't eat them.[15] No great visions to lure them on, only the needs of survival for themselves and their institutions. They may have no clear picture of the world they are destined to inhabit; no total assurance about the future. This is not a fault. The situation is not suited to concentration on one or a very few great visions.

Some Scenarios

I think this absence of assured great visions and a generalized apprehension about the future help to explain why there are so few efforts today to predict the future of higher education and why those that do exist mostly have such a negative cast.

Among the first that came to my attention was one set forth by Michael Shattock of Warwick University in England at the 1991 centennial celebration of the University of Chicago. Shattock saw the possibility of universities going the way of the monasteries at the time of King Henry VIII: destroyed, with their monks driven into the wilderness.[16] This time around Margaret Thatcher was to be Henry VIII. More realistically, Shattock saw external developments gaining more influence over the universities, a stronger role for the government as universities became an "arm of the state," increasing domination by the economic market with the university becoming an arm of industry, reduced financial resources, and the movement of advanced education outside the colleges and universities. He saw, in particular, a great takeover by state and by industry. Gone was the autonomous university of old (Oxford and Cambridge, for example) with the academy in charge of its own future.

Even earlier I had read the comment of Ernest Boyer and Fred Hechinger that higher education in the United States was "no longer at the vital center of the nation's work" as it had been in the 1960s, that it was now "adrift."[17] I agree that it is now adrift, but it may be at the vital center of a society adrift.

Then I read Peter Drucker, who has been so right so many times in his appraisal of future possibilities that one cannot ignore him. He wrote that "long distance learning . . . may well make obsolete in 25 years that unique American institution, the free-standing American college."[18] This would leave mostly the university, which Drucker, however, ominously called "a failure."[19] Currently American higher education is comprised of fifteen million students. Only about 1,800,000, or 12 percent, are graduate students. The other 88 percent are subject, according to Drucker, to the obliteration of "college students" as we have known them. This is a grand hedgehog vision that dwarfs anything in the 1960s.

Arthur Levine has recently predicted that higher education administration will become less the management of campuses, which now total some 3,500, and become more the management of the electronic distribution of knowledge to individual destinations, however remote. The student is driven into the "wilderness."[20]

The most recent commentary I have seen and the broadest in its analysis is by Frank Rhodes of Cornell University provisorily entitled *The American University, Dinosaur or Dynamo?*[21] Rhodes comes out on the side of the dynamo but warns, among other things, of the impacts of diminished resources and the loss of the "monopoly" of advanced education by traditional higher education institutions to institutions like the University of Phoenix with its focus on evening classes and distance learning for working adults..

There are other possible scenarios. I have doubts about all of them, but they do demonstrate the tensions of the period in which we live.

Danger. Before looking at other scenarios, I note that in looking forward, it is important to avoid the big danger of overvaluing the past and undervaluing the future. I have attended dozens of official celebratory occasions of colleges and universities, and I have come to expect references to a "glorious past" and to a "fearsome future." Why is the past always seen as so glorious? In the 20th century, the past mostly *was* glorious. To say so is a way to thank past contributors. It is also a way for current authorities to boast about what they have done. But why is the future always so fearsome? I think:

It often is.

To say that it is so is an argument for making the changes the current authorities see as necessary.

It is also a way to encourage supporters to continue or to increase their support.

If things do go wrong, it then becomes possible for current leaders to say, "I warned you."

If things, however, go right, they can say, "I saved you."

In any event, I have seldom heard it said that the past has been gruesome, but the future is going to be glorious. Robert Gordon Sproul, my long-term predecessor as president of the University of California, once told me his views when I asked his advice about what to talk about on official occasions. He said that there were only four possibilities:

To view the past with pride.

To anticipate the future with apprehension.

To view the past with pride and then anticipate the future with apprehension.

Then he stopped. I asked him "what is the fourth?" He replied, "There is no fourth." I said, "What about lambasting the past and anticipating the future?" He answered, "I have never seen that work." And I have come to agree. To say the past is awful and to promise that the future will be glorious is to boast in advance of performance and to set a standard of improvement that is too high.

There does seem to be a tendency in higher education to view the future with alarm and the past with appreciation. The danger is to overdo it and become paralyzed with fear. I remember in 1960 the fear of increasing enrollment was overwhelming: "more is worse"; and in 1980 we were terrified by the oncoming demographic depression with campus after campus going out of business. Beware the doomsayers. I hope in this essay I have not fallen into the trap of the same old rhetorical game. If I have, you have been warned.

But I do draw five conclusions from this historical record of how gruesome fears have so often and in so many places in retrospect become glorious triumphs:

1. Higher education has been very resilient in turning fears into triumphs. I expect that this will continue. It is due to the angels who march in where fools fear to tread.
2. It is better to concentrate on basic long-term trends and not on current annoyances.
3. The first, best step in conquering the future is to worry about it—to fear it. Worry is the beginning of wisdom.
4. Fear should liberate responses, not imprison them.

5. It is useful to be confident that a glorious past might be followed by a glorious future.

The Methuselah scenario.   In the 1930s when the social security system was established in the United States, we had millions of unemployed workers, and for every person on social security we had twenty in the labor force. In 2030 when the rate of retirement of Baby Boomers reaches its peak, we will have a ratio of only 2 to 1.[22] This may set off a great conflict over the share of the national resources that goes to members of different groups. It will also set off a contest within the group of retirees themselves, who will form a powerful political group. They will want all they can get for themselves today but will also want a fair share for those still in the labor force or who are about to enter it. Their future welfare will depend on the skills and goodwill of these workers. Nasty warfare may take place between the old and the young, parents and children, retired Anglos and labor force minorities.[23] The needs of higher education for youth will be even more in conflict for resources with the need for increased support for the aged.

The DNA revolution.   The biological sciences will be at the center of university life, in medical schools as well as agricultural programs. They will spearhead the invasion of industry into the campus, as physics did the invasion of government and the military over half a century ago. The military brought secret research to academic life. Industry will bring new opportunities for better research but also the potential for interference with academic integrity. But above all, the pursuit of the secrets of DNA will raise widespread ethical issues—a new Pandora's Box. Does the future of human life, and all forms of life, belong with God, the creator, or with Darwin's process of survival of the fittest or with the scientists and their unlimited imaginations? I

remember traveling the state of California talking to public
groups when the secrets of DNA first began to be understood
and hearing the reactions of horror that exceed the fears that
accompanied the explosion of nuclear bombs over Hiroshima
and Nagasaki.

The integrated university in the process of disintegration. The
university was long ago integrated with agriculture and medicine
and law. Then, during World War II, it became integrated with
the military. That process has continued with further integration
with the labor market. Our traditional eighteen to twenty-four-
year old students (Market I) are being supplemented by nontra-
ditional students aged twenty-five to sixty-five (Market II). Market II already constitutes 40 percent of all enrollments on a
head-count basis, and more educational programs for both markets are job-oriented. Education for its own sake is being replaced by education for the sake of employment, as student
curricular choices attest. And a new market (Market III) is being
born for retired persons. The theme of a liberal education for a
well-rounded life fades in all three of these markets, perhaps least
of all for those in Market III who are interested in what they
might have missed along the way.

The ivory tower of old has become an arm of the state and an
arm of industry, and the students inside reach out toward the
labor market and toward political influence. The increasing per-
meability of the ivory tower's walls raises many ethical and
political issues for the academy. How this flow of contacts is
managed will affect the essential nature of the university whose
leaders need to be concerned not only with the inward flow of
state and industry influence, but also with the outward flow of
faculty consultation and student participation in external politics.

Integration into the external world inevitably leads to disintegration of the university internally. What are perceived by some as the injustices in the external labor market penetrate the system of economic rewards on campus, replacing policies of internal justice.[24] Commitments to external interests lead to internal conflicts over the impartiality of the search for truth. Ideologies conflict. Friendships and loyalties flow increasingly outward. Spouses, who once held the academic community together as a social unit, now have their own jobs. "Alma Mater Dear" to whom we "sing a joyful chorus" becomes an almost laughable idea.

The globalization scenario. The globalization of the world economy, with its international flow of communications and transportation, drives some industries into the universities. Access to the newest and best knowledge is the secret to global success for many industries and is best obtained inside the universities where there is the new knowledge and the people who create, share, and learn it. The university does become an arm of industry, although it is inherently strong enough to set its own terms of trade. What it has is very valuable. But it has at least two weaknesses. First, if one university sets strict terms to protect its integrity, another may outbid it and go on to steal its faculty. Second, faculty in internal units with high external value will be tempted to fight for industrial contracts under the banner of departmental autonomy and threaten to move to another less exacting institution if their access is denied. Thus the university's potential bargaining strength is greatly reduced unless there is a compact among universities or, more likely, governmental legislation, setting forth what will and will not be acceptable, and in addition, an oversight mechanism set up by the overall campus faculty to determine what is acceptable and what is not. Otherwise, the university is helpless in the face of the combined onslaught of aggressive industry and entrepreneurial faculty members. At a minimum, universities may wish to set up special agencies to manage the new industrial contracts, as the University of California did in World War II with Livermore and Los Alamos, strictly controlled by the board of trustees.

The fractionalization of the academic guild. (1) Subject matter specialization increases, breaking knowledge into tinier and tinier topics. Once upon a time, the entire academic enterprise originated in and remained connected to philosophy. (2) Conflict advances over the system of monetary rewards between those committed to internal justice among fields and those devoted to following the injustices of the external labor market field by field. (3) Fractionalization also increases over differing convictions about social justice, over whether it should be defined as equality of opportunity or as equality of results, the latter often taking the form of equality of representation. This may turn out to be the penultimate ideological battle on campus. (4) The ultimate conflict may occur over models of the university itself, whether to support the traditional or the "postmodern" model. The traditional model is based on the enlightenment of the eighteenth century—rationality, scientific processes of thought, the search for truth, objectivity, "knowledge for its own sake and for its practical applications." And the traditional university, to quote the Berkeley philosopher John Searle, "attempts to be apolitical or at least politically neutral. The university of postmodernism thinks that all discourse is political anyway, and it seeks to use the university for beneficial rather than repressive political ends . . . The postmodernists are attempting to challenge certain traditional assumptions about the nature of truth, objectivity, rationality, reality, and intellectual quality."[25]

The conflict between adherents of the traditional and the postmodern university is just beginning. It might come to tear apart some of the humanities and some of the social sciences. I note that those most neglected by the modern university, including the literature departments, seem to be the most frequent supporters of the postmodern university, which adds to the tensions.

Any further politicization of the university will, of course, alienate much of the public at large. While most acknowledge that the traditional university was partially politicized already, postmodernism will further raise questions of whether the critical function of the university is based on political orientations rather than on nonpolitical scientific analysis. Since the traditional university is a child of the enlightenment and, in fact, is also its major instrument of advancement, any effective attack on it by the proponents of the postmodern university will be enormously important.

The free-for-all scenario. This is a Hobbesian world of each against all and of all against each where life is "nasty, brutish, and short": the state against the campus, industry against the campus, new technology versus old, old people versus young, friends and enemies of the DNA revolution, supporters and detractors of the traditional university, among other conflicts. One can imagine some twenty-first century Luddites fighting against the obsolescence of their skills and the extinction of their livelihood. Disunity triumphs across the board.

All these scenarios have their negative aspects. None is fully welcomed by the academic community. Let me add one that is widely welcome: a continuation of the status quo of 2000. Campuses still have a degree of autonomy if they choose to exercise it. Faculty still have some essential control over academic affairs. Faculty income mostly permits an affluent way of life. Faculty members have remarkable management of their working times and conditions. It may well be that Shangri La is here and now, startling as that observation may be! And perhaps it will never come again. There is no way to turn back the power of the state or of industry, or the electronic and DNA revolutions, or much else that is now going on. While it lasts, however, we might come to welcome "the heaven on earth" not yet lost. The best is here and now. The perpetuation of the "here and now" becomes the final rallying cry of conservative academics.

And there are the utopian scenarios: the accumulated knowledge of all the civilizations of the world at the click of a button to the most remote person on the planet, the obliteration of the most feared diseases, and the creation of a world with sustenance for all.

Some Certainties

Yet, even in a chaotic world, there may be some certainties on which to build, even without the great imperatives that characterized the 1960s.

OLD BUSINESS

This includes some unfinished business of the twentieth century to be completed in the twenty-first:

Extending more opportunities to historical minorities. In California, for example, there have been movements backward since the Master Plan of 1960, including enormous discrepancies in the availability of advanced placement courses in high schools and transfer programs in community colleges between low-income and high-income neighborhoods, discrepancies that increase inequalities of opportunity.[26] Public universities in some states (including California, Texas, and Florida) face a demographic revolution as historical minorities expand in size and in political power. How will they adapt?

Offering more help to primary and secondary education. I know of no school of education that has distinguished itself in this endeavor, although some have tried valiantly. I suggest that these colleges try a land-grant instead of a letters and science approach, with experiment stations and extension services, rather than affiliations with the literature of the standard departments such as history, philosophy, and psychology. I also suggest more experimentation with full-time, full-service primary and secondary schools, as so many families reduce their educational functions—schools open, for example, from 7 A.M. to 7 P.M. with eating facilities, libraries, recreational programs, and medical facilities, among other services. I think that too much blame is being placed on the schools and too little on the deterioration of education within families. The family failed before the schools failed.

New Business

Several items of new business are already on the agenda:

Using information technology more widely and more effectively. This is the fourth revolution in the technology of education and the first in 500 years. The first came as specialized teachers or tutors supplemented the teaching of children by families and of apprentices by journeymen, as sedentary agriculture and cities replaced a nomadic existence. The second revolution, writing, occurred at about the same time as the first, the third with the printing press, and now the fourth with electronic communications. Each of these revolutions has evolved as an add-on, not as a total replacement, as was the case of the automobile taking the place of the horse and buggy completely. I expect that electronic technology will also be an add-on and not a low-cost total replacement for hands-on education as some public authorities seem to hope in their plans for "virtual universities." The big test will be quality and not cost alone, and quality is very costly.

I realize that with interactive technology people can have fairly satisfactory human contact at some distance from one another—can see, hear, and converse with one another and among groups from separate locations. Also, e-mail has been found sometimes to encourage debate and add to motivation by increasing faculty accessibility. But education has long been a hands-on enterprise, as are other ancient professions such as medicine, law, and theology, dealing with different individuals with different needs that are not subject to standardized treatment.

Once I identified eighty-five institutions that had been in existence since 1520 and were still largely unchanged. Seventy of them were universities.[27] Universities are among the most conservative of all institutions in their methods of governance and conduct and are likely to remain so. In addition, students learn from each other and not just from teachers or computers, and there is as yet no substitute for face-to-face contact with other students. I do, nevertheless, see a vast expansion of local learning campuses such as the University of the Highlands and Islands in Scotland, Washington State University, and many others in the United States, which use the video lecture, for example, as one basis for subsequent direct discussions among students under the guidance of a seminar chairperson. Discussion leaders may replace lecturers of particular subjects, particularly in large-scale and standardized courses for lower-level students. The one-room primary school may be replaced by the one-room university, but what about laboratories?

If the electronic revolution does turn out to be a total replacement for classroom lectures instead of primarily an add-on, then it could become the great theme for the next century—the end of lecturing to undergraduates as seen by Peter Drucker. But we need much more experimentation before that conclusion can be reached. Education is not only about the transfer of factual knowledge, but also about learning to reach conclusions with others.

Continuation of the rise of the biological sciences. The biological sciences are becoming a center for all university science fields, drawing into their area of influence medicine, engineering, physics, chemistry, and much else. They now receive the most federal, philanthropic, and industrial support and are becoming the greatest sources of change in society and the biggest sources of ethical conflicts in the new century. Leadership in the biological sciences will be necessary for any research university that aspires to greatness in the twenty-first century. Here is another possible theme for the coming century.

Higher education as preparation for mid-career advancement. Mid-career advancement is bound to become more important as occupational skill levels continue to rise and as high-skill occupations multiply. Corporate classrooms and institutions like the University of Phoenix have led the way. I am sure there is much to follow, particularly in the area of medical care where so many new skills at the highest levels are desperately needed.[28] Higher education, so enlarged, will become even more of an appendage of the labor market. American higher education began as an effort at moral uplift. It continues as an effort to get a good or better job. A life of affluence is replacing a philosophy of life as the main purpose of higher education. Another rising market (Market III) serves retired persons wanting education. Higher education, work, and leisure are being scrambled according to many new recipes. Higher education is less an institution apart and is integrated into all industrial and social life. Markets II and III may be particularly appropriate for electronic education off campus.

Consequences of the labor market's increasing domination of

higher education include divergent views about the best undergraduate curriculum or no concern at all with so-called "liberal
education." Another consequence is to redefine governance from
a common concern for the welfare of the whole campus to
divided concerns for its constituent parts. Some units even toy
with privatization.

Further integration into society spells further disintegration
within the campus. External societal pressures sharpen the challenge for academic leaders to maintain their own sense of direction and their own sense of values. The more the university is
seen as a collection of instruments to help this or that interest in
society, the harder presidents and faculty leaders will have to
work to set their own priorities, to assert the university's independence, to determine how they may best serve the general
welfare, and to decide how best to govern themselves and not
be totally influenced by others. As the institutional borders of
higher education become more permeable, the control of traffic
back and forth demands more scrutiny by administrative and
academic leaders. Control of this flow is central to control of the
nature of the university. The drawbridge is now down. Who and
what shall cross over it?

SOME REPERCUSSIONS
These several items of old and new business are bringing, in their
turn, some necessary adaptations.

The role of the president is changing. He or she now courts
wealth more off campus—even sells parts of the campus: Campus"x".com. When the president is at home, he or she still
worries about preserving a sense of community but does not
know exactly how that might be done and turns to dreams of
"big rock candy mountains."

Further integration into society inevitably increases the role of the boards of trustees and government agencies and other groups that represent the interests of the external society, and reduces the role of the faculty, which is concerned about internal guild interests. Using the terminology of Henry Rosovsky, there are now many more "owners" of parts of the university.[29] Selecting, training, and guiding these owners becomes crucial to the welfare of higher education.

New resources, in recent times, have been becoming harder to obtain and thus the effective use of resources becomes a more central concern. Economic growth has slowed as the rate of increases in productivity has fallen from 3 percent in the 1960s to 2 percent in the 1970s and 1 percent in the 1980s, although rising again to 3 percent in the late 1990s. The return to a 3 percent rate of productivity increase may prove to be not a long-term development, but only a one-time shot in the arm. At the same time, competitive demands for these resources have grown, and they are here to stay. As a consequence, the more effective use of resources will become a more dominant concern, and it is a more natural concern of trustees and governors than of academic senates. Admission policies and tuition levels also have become public concerns and therefore also trustee and state government concerns. The distribution of power will be greatly affected.

Different segments of higher education are being and will be affected differently by changing circumstances. The best of the liberal arts colleges are likely to be the least affected by the new electronic technology since they are mostly engaged in the all-around development of children of the already affluent (the top one-fifth of the economic scale), providing sports, lifetime friends, social skills, programs for cultural interests, and all-around intellectual advancement, not just job skills. These institutions get their main support from gifts by affluent alumni who have the ability and the willingness to pay high tuitions for their children, not from public funds.

Also little affected by the new technology will be graduate work in the research universities and even some undergraduate instruction. It is hands-on apprenticeship that cannot be replaced by electronics. But these universities will be most affected by the DNA revolution.

The teaching of large undergraduate classes in state and community colleges may be most affected by the new technology. So also may be the demand for discussion leaders in off-campus learning centers supplementing electronic presentations in the chat rooms.

Total enrollments in all forms of higher education will continue to rise but may be more subject to short-term fluctuations, as the rate of return to a college education falls and rises and as opportunities for career advancement fluctuate with the economy. In contrast, in earlier centuries access to class status was a more stable basis for enrollments than are current labor market fluctuations.

Each of these certainties has within it a number of uncertainties. And there will be wild cards ahead, such as wars and depressions, that no one can foresee today.

It is going to be increasingly difficult, I think, to speak about higher education as a single entity.

Wild Cards

Let me mention a few possible wild cards, in addition to wars and depressions. First, what will happen to increases in productivity in the future; and, second, what will happen to fluctuations in returns to a higher education?

A third wild card is how well the United States will fare in the global economy, as other nations or unions of nations (for example, the EU) may catch up with and even surpass it. The quality of education and training for all citizens will be central to this contest. The American university may no longer be supreme.

Fourth, new episodes of student unrest may occur. Students may once again seek to assert the role of the university as independent critic. Of course, labor market concerns may become too obsessive for this to happen—too many upwardly mobile students and too few well-educated downwardly mobile.

A fifth wild card is how the various battles within the professoriate will turn out, the battle over academic merit versus social justice in treatment of students, over internal justice in the professional reward system versus the pressures of external markets, over the better model for the university—modern versus postmodern.

Big worry. In addition to my concerns about whether the foxes or the hedgehogs will assume presidential leadership and how well they will use it, I worry about the central mechanisms that make decisions about higher education. Will the members of increasingly externally-oriented boards of trustees, coordinating councils, legislatures, and governors' offices be sufficiently flexible, devoted, and possessed of enough wisdom to guide institutions through the troubles ahead? The most critical pressures will be on those who handle the flow of transactions between universities and the external society's power centers. Will they know enough, care enough, be vested with sufficient high-level, long-term judgment to manage the flow effectively? By the nature of the situations, these mechanisms, and those who manage them, will be at the center of the storms. They should receive early and critical scrutiny. And internal faculty organizations will need to be in closer touch with external forces than historically has been the case. They should develop capabilities to respond faster and more effectively than in the past.

Conclusion. Through all these changes and challenges, the fox may be in its element; only the fox is alert enough, clever enough, agile enough, not blinded by big visions, survivalist enough to make its way through all the complexities, all the traps. I hope, however, the fox will have a few hedgehogs around to remind it to protect university autonomy and the authority of faculty senates and to assert the importance of public as well as guild welfare.

I know of only one recent observer of American higher education who has taken what I consider to be both a possibly realistic and a clearly benign hedgehog's view of the future of higher education: Howard Bowen. Two decades ago he set forth a vision of a "nation of educated people" taking better care of their health, investing their wealth more effectively, behaving more efficiently as consumers, developing more fully their economic skills, and participating more widely and more wisely in political and cultural life.[30] His scenario is my favorite.

Bowen was one of the last of the optimistic hedgehogs. When he was still alive, he and I used to talk of ourselves as among the remnants of the great optimists of the 1960s, with our tunnel visions of a better world through the efforts of the modern university—a threatened species still pursuing the Holy Grail. Bowen, in developing his vision, drew on his book for the Carnegie Council on the proven benefits of higher education, *Investment in Learning,* plus the fact that we are still moving in the direction of universal participation in education beyond the high school level—60 percent perhaps increasing to 70 or 80 percent.[31]

If I were, however, a fox in the year 2000 looking around me trying to see what was going on, I would concentrate on the following (I realize that many of the following items existed in 1960 although in very subdued forms):

The globalization of economic markets and their impact on the American economy and on higher education.

The fluctuation in the rates of productivity increases.

The fluctuation in rates of economic returns to a college education.

The new market of middle-aged students seeking job advancement (Market II).

The changing demographics among state populations.

The new electronic technology.

The rise in dominance of the biological sciences, and the intensity and direction of public reaction to their discoveries.

The ongoing battles within the unhappy humanities, and between supporters of the traditional and the postmodern models of the university and other internecine conflicts.

The further integration of higher education into labor markets and into industry, and the resultant disintegration of the once self-contained campus.

The rise of for-profit competitors to nonprofit higher education.

The movement of more governing power into the hands of non-academic authorities, particularly governors and trustees.

Battles between internal and external powers over the more effective use of resources.

The behavior of the aging population towards its younger members, and vice versa.

The lessened prestige and public standing of the cities of intellect since the 1960s when they were at their peak of public favor and influence.

Wars and depressions, student unrest, and other wild cards.

There are many things occurring, not one or two big things, all at once and with and against each other—a natural habitat for the fox. So many voices compete with so little wisdom. It is a tougher context to work through than in the 1960s, with a lesser flow of economic resources.

I would have at least three wishes as a fox:

1. That careful studies would continue to be made of the new information technologies—what is working and what is not? But, with new products coming along faster than old products can be tested, this process is greatly handicapped.
2. That an open, in-depth debate would take place between proponents of the traditional and the postmodern university instead of the sniper shots of guerilla warfare. Postmodernism is gaining ground but without a fair frontal confrontation—more and more islands of postmodernism in a hostile sea.
3. That an in-depth discussion would take place about the ethical systems of the future university. The last accepted code of ethics was set forth by the American Association of University Professors almost a century ago. The AAUP looked at internal ethical problems relating to the proper domains of trustees, presidents, and faculties. Now the ethical problems are found more in the flow of contacts between the academic and the external worlds. There have never been so many ethical problems swirling about as today.

Finally, Ken Galbraith once spoke of two kinds of economists. One type included those who acknowledge "I don't know"—the good guys. The other kind consisted of those who "don't know they don't know"—the bad guys. I hope that, at a minimum, I have demonstrated that I belong to the former type. I don't know but I am curious. I don't know but I think I know enough to remove the question mark from the title of this essay and replace it with an exclamation point—"a century for the foxes!" We need the foxes looking all around them at many things, large and small.

What incredible opportunities these foxes have to explore the intricacies of a century of so many discontinuities, of so many alternative scenarios, of so many opportunities to turn challenges into triumphs, and of so many opportunities to explore and create solutions.

To the hedgehogs of the 1960s of which I was one: rest in peace; to the foxes of the twenty-first century: great expectations for success in your attempted escapes from the maze!

NOTES

PREFACE, 2001

1. *"By adding a single sentence, Kerr's book would become the work of a proto-fascist ideologue."* [Emphasis in original.] Hal Draper, "The Mind of Clark Kerr," in Draper, *Berkeley: The New Student Revolt* (New York: Grove Press, 1965), p. 212.

2. Henry Rosovsky, *The University: An Owner's Manual* (New York: W. W. Norton, 1990), p. 297.

1. THE IDEA OF A MULTIVERSITY

1. John Henry Cardinal Newman, *The Idea of a University* (New York: Longmans Green and Co., 1947). The quotations used here are from pp. 129, 91, xxvii, 157.

2. Francis Bacon, "The Advancement of Learning," *Essays, Advance of Learning, New Atlantis and Other Places* (New York: Odyssey Press, Inc., 1937), pp. 214–215.

3. Abraham Flexner, *Universities: American English German* (New York: Oxford University Press, 1930). The quotations are from pp. 3, 4, 42, 179, 132, 25, 44–45, 197, 193, 231, 235, 197 (again), 178–179.

4 Harvard University, *The President's Report, 1961–62*, p. 3

5. Hastings Rashdall, *The Universities of Europe in the Middle*

Ages (3 vols., 1895, ed. F. M. Powicke and A. B. Emden, Oxford: Clarendon Press, 1936), III, 358.

6. Benjamin Franklin, *Proposals Relating to the Education of Youth in Pensilvania* (Philadelphia, 1749).

7. *Reports of the Course of Instruction in Yale College by a Committee of the Corporation and the Academical Faculty* (New Haven, Conn.: Hezekiah Howe, 1828).

8. Allan Nevins, *The State Universities and Democracy* (Urbana: University of Illinois Press, 1962), p. vi.

9. John J. Corson, *Governance of Colleges and Universities* (New York: McGraw-Hill, 1960), pp. 175–179.

10. José Ortega y Gasset, *The Mission of the University* (London: Kegan Paul, Trench, Trubner and Co., Ltd., 1946), p. 56.

11. McGeorge Bundy, "Of Winds and Windmills: Free Universities and Public Policy," in Charles G. Dobbins, ed., *Higher Education and the Federal Government, Programs and Problems* (Washington, D.C.: American Council on Education, 1963), p. 93.

12. *General Education in a Free Society,* Report of the Harvard Committee with an Introduction by James Bryant Conant (Cambridge, Mass.: Harvard University Press, 1945).

13. Richard Hofstadter and Walter P. Metzger, *The Development of Academic Freedom in the United States* (New York: Columbia University Press, 1955), pp. 71, 61.

14. Thorstein Veblen, *The Higher Learning in America* (Stanford, Calif.: Academic Reprints, 1954), p. 85.

15. Upton Sinclair, *The Goose-Step: A Study of American Education* (Pasadena: John Regan & Co., 1923), pp. 382–384.

16. Robert Maynard Hutchins, *Freedom, Education and The Fund: Essays and Addresses, 1946–1956* (New York: Meridian Books, 1956), pp. 167–196.

17. Harold W. Dodds, *The Academic President—Educator or Caretaker?* (New York: McGraw-Hill, 1962).

18. Frederick Rudolph, *The American College and University: A History* (New York: Alfred A. Knopf, 1962), p. 492.

19. James Lewis Morrill, *The Ongoing State University* (Minneapolis: University of Minnesota Press, 1960), p. 48.

20. John D. Millett, *The Academic Community: An Essay on Organization* (New York: McGraw-Hill, 1962), p. 259.
21. Henry M. Wriston, *Academic Procession: Reflections of a College President* (New York: Columbia University Press, 1959), p. 172.
22. Eric Ashby, "The Administrator: Bottleneck or Pump?" *Daedalus*, Spring 1962, pp. 264–278.
23. Hutchins, pp. 177, 169.
24. A. Lawrence Lowell, *What a University President Has Learned* (New York: Macmillan, 1938), pp. 12, 19.
25. Rudolph, p. 291.
26. James Morris, "Is Oxford Out of This World?" *Horizon*, January 1963, p. 86.
27. James Bryce, *The American Commonwealth*, new edition (New York: Macmillan, 1914), II, 718–719.
28. Paul F. Lazarsfeld, "The Sociology of Empirical Social Research," *American Sociological Review*, December 1962, pp. 751–767.
29. David Riesman, *Constraint and Variety in American Education* (Garden City, N.Y.: Doubleday, 1958), pp. 30–32.
30. Ernest Earnest, *Academic Procession* (Indianapolis: Bobbs-Merrill, 1953), p. 74.
31. Rudolph, p. 423.
32. Eric Ashby, "Self-Government in Modern British Universities," *Science and Freedom*, December 1956, p. 10.
33. Theodore Caplow and Reece J. McGee, *The Academic Marketplace* (New York: Basic Books, 1958), p. 206.
34. Millett, p. 224.
35. Wriston, p. 172.
36. Nevins, pp. 118–119.
37. Dodds, p. 43.
38. W. Max Wise, *They Come For the Best of Reasons—College Students Today* (Washington, D.C.: American Council on Education, 1958).
39. Burton R. Clark and Martin Trow, *Determinants of College Student Subculture*, unpublished manuscript, Center for the Study of Higher Education, University of California, Berkeley, 1963.

40. Robert Bendiner, "The Non-Teacher," *Horizon,* September 1962, p. 14.
41. Merle A. Tuve, "Is Science Too Big for the Scientist?" *Saturday Review,* June 6, 1959, p. 49.

2. The Realities of the Federal Grant University

1. Don K. Price, "The Scientific Establishment," *Science,* June 29, 1962.
2. Some of the principal reports, 1960–1963, are as follows:

American Assembly, *The Federal Government and Higher Education* (Englewood Cliffs, N.J.: Prentice-Hall, 1960).

Homer D. Babbidge, Jr., and Robert M. Rosenzweig, *The Federal Interest in Higher Education* (New York: McGraw-Hill, 1962).

William G. Bowen, *The Federal Government and Princeton University: A Report on the Effects of Princeton's Involvements with the Federal Government on the Operations of the University* (Princeton University, 1962).

Julius H. Comroe, Jr., ed., *Research and Medical Education* (Evanston, Ill.: Association of American Medical Colleges, 1962).

Charles G. Dobbins, ed., *Higher Education and the Federal Government, Programs and Problems* (Washington, D.C.: American Council on Education, 1963).

Harvard and the Federal Government: A Report to the Faculties and Governing Boards of Harvard University (Harvard University, September 1961).

Charles V. Kidd, *American Universities and Federal Research* (Cambridge, Mass.: The Belknap Press of Harvard University Press, 1959).

J. Kenneth Little, *A Survey of Federal Programs in Higher Education: Summary Describing the Programs, Participating Institutions, and the Effects of the Programs on the Institutions* (Washington, D.C.: Government Printing Office, 1962).

Harold Orlans, *The Effects of Federal Programs on Higher*

Education: A Study of 36 Universities and Colleges (Washington, D.C.: Brookings Institution, 1962).

Alice M. Rivlin, *The Role of the Federal Government in Financing Higher Education* (Washington, D.C.: Brookings Institution, 1961).

Glenn T. Seaborg *et al., Scientific Progress, the Universities and the Federal Government: A Statement by the President's Science Advisory Committee,* Nov. 15, 1960.

3. These fourteen specialized research centers are:

Columbia Radiation Laboratory (Columbia)—Department of Defense.

Applied Physics Laboratory (Johns Hopkins)—Department of the Navy.

Hudson Laboratories (Columbia)—Department of the Navy.

Lincoln Laboratory (M.I.T.)—Department of the Air Force.

Argonne National Laboratory (Chicago)—Atomic Energy Commission.

Cambridge Electron Accelerator (Harvard and M.I.T.)—Atomic Energy Commission.

Lawrence Radiation Laboratory (California)—Atomic Energy Commission.

Los Alamos Scientific Laboratory (California)—Atomic Energy Commission.

Princeton-Pennsylvania Proton Accelerator (Princeton and Pennsylvania)—Atomic Energy Commission.

Princeton Stellerator (Princeton)—Atomic Energy Commission.

Jet Propulsion Laboratory (California Institute of Technology)—National Aeronautics and Space Administration.

Brookhaven National Laboratory (Associated Universities, Inc.)—National Science Foundation.

Kitt Peak Observatory (Association of Universities for Research in Astronomy)—National Science Foundation.

Green Bank Radio Astronomy Observatory (Associated Universities, Inc.)—National Science Foundation and Department of the Air Force.

4. Sidney Hook, "The Impact of Expanding Research Support on the Universities," in Comroe, ed., pp. 235–237.

5. Malcolm Moos and Francis E. Rourke, *The Campus and the State* (Baltimore: Johns Hopkins Press, 1959).

6. See James B. Handler, "An Optimistic View," in Comroe, ed., p. 108: "When asked, they much prefer judgment by a jury in Washington to the risk of judgment by colleagues at home."

7. Homer D. Babbidge, Jr., and Robert M. Rosenzweig, "The Issues," *The Graduate Journal,* University of Texas, vol. V (1962), Supplement, pp. 62–104.

8. Dael Wolfle, *America's Resources of Specialized Talent* (New York: Harper, 1954), pp. 190–191, 317–322.

9. Orlans, p. 173.

10. Hook, p. 238.

11. Orlans, p. 134.

12. J. A. Stratton, "Research and the University," *Chemical and Engineering News,* vol. 31, no. 25 (June 22, 1953), pp. 2582–2583.

13. Nathan Pusey, "The Carnegie Study," in Dobbins, ed., p. 25.

14. Don K. Price, *Government and Science* (New York: New York University Press, 1954), p. 96.

15. Logan Wilson, "A New Dimension," *The Graduate Journal,* University of Texas, vol. V (1962), Supplement, p. 164.

16. Seaborg *et al.,* as cited in note 2, above. See also in this connection the Report of the President's Science Advisory Committee, *Meeting Manpower Needs in Science and Technology: Graduate Training in Engineering, Mathematics, and Physical Sciences,* Dec. 12, 1962.

17. Roswell L. Gilpatric, *The Changing Patterns of Defense Procurement,* issued by the Office of the Secretary of Defense, June 19, 1962.

18. *Circular Letter No. 4,* Association of State Universities and Land-Grant Colleges (Washington, D.C., Feb. 13, 1963).

19. "The situation appears to call for general aid to U.S. universities patterned somewhat after that provided universities in the United Kingdom by the University Grants Committee. In any event, the question arises of direct subsidy to educational institutions in

order to increase the over-all strength of their departments and to provide greater flexibility in their administration." National Science Foundation, *Annual Report, 1960*, p. 16.

Also, Sidney Hook, in Comroe, ed., p. 245, says, "Personally, I see the best solution—not the ideal solution, for there is none—in the system that today obtains in England, where through the University Grants Committee the government makes lump grants to universities that are not earmarked for specific purposes. This system would give a university the necessary autonomy to meet educational needs as it sees them, and permit the deployment of resources at the key points of its educational enterprise."

20. John Walsh, "Congress: Lag in Science Advice Gives Executive an Advantage," *Science*, vol. 139, no. 3549 (Jan. 4, 1963), p. 27.

21. *Harvard and the Federal Government*, p. 26.

22. Basil O'Connor, "Science and Government—The Perilous Partnership," speech delivered Jan. 16, 1963, at the Third Symposium on Immunopathology, La Jolla, Calif.

23. President John F. Kennedy, *Message on Education*, Jan. 29, 1963.

24. Orlans, p. 169. It might be noted that the designations "public" and "private" have considerably less meaning for the federal grant universities than they once did for institutions of higher education.

25. Orlans, p. 264.

26. Charles V. Kidd, "The Institute Discussion: Research Emphasis and Research Itself," in Comroe, ed., p. 120.

27. Orlans, p. 180.

28. Alvin M. Weinberg, "Criteria for Scientific Choice," *Minerva*, Winter 1962.

29. See *Report to the President on Government Contracting for Research and Development*, prepared by the Bureau of the Budget and referred to the Committee on Government Operations, United States Senate, May 17, 1962; and *Operation and Management of Research and Development Facilities and Programs, Analytical and Advisory Services and Technical Supervision of Weapons Systems and Other Programs for the Gov-*

ernment, In-House and by Contract, prepared by a committee under the chairmanship of Helge Holst, treasurer and corporate counsel of Arthur D. Little, Inc., and dated April 17, 1962.

30. See the White House special message, *Improving American Health,* Feb. 7, 1963.
31. American Assembly (note 2, above), p. 199.
32. McGeorge Bundy, "Of Winds and Windmills: Free Universities and Public Policy," in Dobbins, ed. (note 2, above), pp. 96–98.

3. THE FUTURE OF THE CITY OF INTELLECT

1. Archibald MacLeish, *The Next Harvard* (Cambridge, Mass.: Harvard University Press, 1941), p. 4.
2. Edward F. Denison, *Sources of Economic Growth in the United States* (New York: Committee for Economic Development, 1962).
3. Fritz Machlup, *The Production and Distribution of Knowledge in the United States* (Princeton, N.J.: Princeton University Press, 1962), pp. 374, 399.
4. Roswell L. Gilpatric, *The Changing Patterns of Defense Procurement,* issued by the Office of the Secretary of Defense, June 19, 1962, p. 7.
5. John Fischer, "The Editor's Easy Chair," *Harper's Magazine,* September 1961, pp. 10–16.
6. Allan Nevins, *The State Universities and Democracy* (Urbana: University of Illinois Press, 1962), p. 114.
7. C. P. Snow, 110th anniversary banquet speech, Washington University, St. Louis, Mo., Feb. 23, 1963.
8. Jacques Barzun, *The House of Intellect* (New York: Harper, 1959).
9. F. M. Cornford, *Microcosmographia Academica: Being a Guide for the Young Academic Politician* (Cambridge, Eng.: Dunster House, 1923), p. 32.
10. Harold Laski, "The American College President," *Harper's Monthly Magazine,* February 1932, p. 319; Abraham Flexner, *Universities: American English German* (New York: Oxford University Press, 1930), p. 5.
11. Frederick Rudolph, *The American College and University: A History* (New York: Alfred A. Knopf, 1962), p. 491.

12. Nevitt Sanford, "Higher Education as a Social Problem," in Sanford, ed., *The American College: A Psychological and Social Interpretation of the Higher Learning* (New York: John Wiley & Sons, 1962), p. 19.

13. C. P. Snow, *The Masters* (New York: Macmillan, 1951), Appendix, p. 382.

14. Eric Ashby, "Self-Government in Modern British Universities," *Science and Freedom,* December 1956, p. 10.

15. Frank Pinner, "The Crisis of the State Universities: Analysis and Remedies," in Sanford, ed., p. 91.

16. Logan Wilson, *Academic Man* (London: Oxford University Press, 1942), p. 71.

17. Ashby, p. 5.

18. *Reports of the Course of Instruction in Yale College by a Committee of the Corporation and the Academical Faculty* (New Haven, Conn.: Hezekiah Howe, 1828), in *American Journal of Science and Arts,* vol. 15 (January 1829), p. 298.

19. J. Robert Oppenheimer, "Science and the Human Community," in Charles Frankel, ed., *Issues in University Education* (New York: Harper, 1959), pp. 56, 58.

20. Beardsley Ruml, *Memo to A College Trustee: A Report on Financial and Structural Problems of the Liberal College* (New York: McGraw-Hill, 1959).

21. Cornford, p. 4.

22. James Bryant Conant, *Education in A Divided World* (Cambridge, Mass.: Harvard University Press, 1949), pp. 158, 171.

23. John Maynard Keynes, *The General Theory* (New York: Harcourt Brace, 1936), p. 383.

24. David Riesman, *Constraint and Variety in American Education* (Garden City, N.Y.: Doubleday, 1958), p. 33.

25. C. P. Snow, *The Two Cultures and the Scientific Revolution* (New York: Cambridge University Press, 1959).

26. Karl Jaspers, *The Idea of the University,* trans. H. A. T. Reiche and H. F. Vanderschmidt (Boston: Beacon Press, 1959), 46.

27. Sir Walter Moberly, *The Crisis in the University* (London: SCM Press, 1949), p. 20.

28. George W. Beadle, "The University of X," *Context,* Fall 1961.

29. Riesman, p. 64.
30. Lee DuBridge, "The Shape of the Future," *Engineering and Science,* California Institute of Technology, February 1962, p. 13.
31. Clark Kerr, John T. Dunlop, Frederick H. Harbison, and Charles A. Myers, *Industrialism and Industrial Man* (Cambridge, Mass.: Harvard University Press, 1960).
32. A. N. Whitehead, *The Aims of Education & Other Essays* (New York: Macmillan, 1929), pp. 22–23.

4. RECONSIDERATIONS AFTER THE REVOLTS OF
THE 1960'S

1. Daniel Bell in *Public Interest,* Fall 1968.
2. Nathan Glazer, *Remembering the Answers* (New York: Basic Books, 1970), p. 215.
3. ". . . the institution is more a 'multiversity' than a 'university' in the older and simpler sense of the word." James Lewis Morrill, *The Ongoing State University* (Minneapolis: University of Minnesota Press, 1960), Preface (n.p.). Virgil Hancher of the University of Iowa, I understand, had also used the word.
4. Alexander G. Ruthven, long-time president of the University of Michigan, once wrote that "alma mater" had become a "crowded smorgasbord." *Naturalist in Two Worlds* (Ann Arbor: University of Michigan Press, 1963), p. 91.
5. William James, *A Pluralistic Universe* (New York: Longmans, Green, and Co., 1909).
6. James, p. 114.
7. James, pp. 321, 325.
8. James A. Perkins sets a higher goal of "coherence" where "all the university's activities advance its capabilities to pursue each of its missions." *The University in Transition* (Princeton: Princeton University Press, 1966), p. 49. A still higher goal might be congruence in the sense of harmony and unity.
9. James, pp. 321–322, 324.
10. J. Douglas Brown, *The Liberal University* (New York: McGraw-Hill Book Co., 1969).
11. Edgar Z. Friedenberg, "L.A. of the Intellect," *New York Review of Books* 1:6 (November 14, 1963), p. 12.

12. Thus professors from UCLA and London (the most multi-multiversity of them all) can write of the "Clark Kerr monstrosity." James M. Buchanan and Nicos E. Devletoglou, *Academia in Anarchy: An Economic Diagnosis* (New York: Basic Books, 1970), p. 177.

13. He also wrote, "Compromise and mediation are inseparable from the pluralistic philosophy." *A Pluralistic Universe,* p. 313. In *Pragmatism, A New Name for Some Old Ways of Thinking* (New York: Longmans, Green, and Co., 1907), p. 40, James writes of the "mediating way of thinking."

14. Ruthven wrote of his years at the University of Michigan that he filled "the role of mediator" and was, of necessity, "continuously in hot water." He said that the president "stands, or should stand, squarely between the staff and the trustees and between the deans of the different schools and colleges." Ruthven, p. 35.

15. Christopher Jencks and David Riesman wrote about *The Uses of the University* as a "much maligned but marvelously perceptive study" and noted how some faculty members "reacted with horror at the mirror . . . held up to them." *The Academic Revolution* (New York: Doubleday and Co., 1968), p. 17.

16. For such a "political" review see "Berkeley and the Fate of the Multiversity" by Sheldon Wolin and John Schaar (*The New York Review of Books,* March 11, 1965). See also my reply, "On Berkeley and the Multiversity" (*The New York Review of Books,* April 8, 1965).

17. Partial contents of this planned chapter later appeared, in somewhat different form, as "Toward the More Perfect University," in *The University in America,* Center for the Study of Democratic Institutions, proceedings of a conference held in Los Angeles in June 1966.

5. ATTEMPTED REFORMS THAT FAILED

1. Carnegie Council on Policy Studies in Higher Education, *A Classification of Institutions of Higher Education,* revised edition (Berkeley: Carnegie Council, 1976).

   The most selective of the liberal arts colleges (Liberal Arts I in the Carnegie classification) also changed relatively little. They also were not deluged by students, had substantial institutional autonomy, were under strong faculty control, and received substantial financial support with freedom to spend it as they saw fit. Some of the less selective liberal arts colleges (Liberal Arts II) changed greatly in efforts to survive. The other institutions (mostly doctoral granting universities, state colleges and universities, and community colleges) were in between, not threatened in their survival but subject to absorbing many more students, with less autonomy from state and local control, with less authority lodged in their organized faculties, with more dependence on the current student market, with more responsibility to meet the demands of the many new, and lesser, professions and occupations. The research universities, by contrast, were more under guild control, more tied to less changing older and more elite functions, and less affected by the new occupations and the new student clienteles.

2. I am choosing my words carefully. I say "intended" in the sense of planned by the institution in advance, as compared with adjustments made in response to political or market pressures, and also in the sense of requiring action by the institution above the level of the individual faculty member or the individual department. I say "internally originated" to contrast with changes externally imposed or influenced. I say "academic" to indicate affecting instruction. I say "structural" to mean doing things in a different way and to exclude changed content in courses which goes on all the time. I say "changes" as a more neutral word than reform, which carries the implication that it is better in some way than what it replaces.

3. I was much interested in a number of changes which were then attempted. Particularly, I was concerned about giving more attention to undergraduate students in research universities, creating more of a sense of an academic community, reducing the fractionalization of the intellectual world, adding more options for the more diversified students to choose among. Also, I felt that experimentation gave a sense of life and dynamism to the academic endeavor; that it drew forth energy and enthusiasm—as in the Hawthorne experiments in industry; that it

served as a check and balance against the old ways of doing things; that it released some faculty and students from their sense of frustration and impotence. I was opposed, however, to changes which reduced academic quality (such as academic credit for experience), which repudiated the value of cognitive learning (such as emphases on affective, "touchy-feely" experiences) and which led to excessive early specialized vocationalism.

4. Gerald Grant and David Riesman, *The Perpetual Dream: Reform and Experiment in the American College* (Chicago: University of Chicago Press, 1978), p. 296.

5. Carnegie Commission on Higher Education, *Less Time, More Options* (New York: McGraw-Hill, 1970).

6. Ann Heiss, *An Inventory of Academic Innovation and Reform* (Berkeley: Carnegie Commission on Higher Education, 1973), discussed innovations adopted in the late 1960's and early 1970's, but at a time too close to their inception to estimate their survival rates. For a description and evaluation of thirteen major curriculum reforms, over half of which are still in existence, see Arthur Levine, *Handbook on Undergraduate Curriculum* (San Francisco: Jossey-Bass, 1978), chapter 13. Levine chose to consider the more permanent of the attempted changes. See also Levine, *Why Innovation Fails* (Albany: State University of New York Press, 1980).

7. A review of forty years of research on methods of teaching concluded that "no particular method of teaching is measurably to be preferred over another when evaluated by student examination performances." Robert Dubin and Thomas C. Taveggia, *The Teaching-Learning Paradox: A Comparative Analysis of College Teaching Methods* (Eugene, Ore.: Center for the Advanced Study of Educational Administration, 1968), p. 31.

8. For a detailed discussion of the elements of academic change in the late nineteenth century, see Laurence R. Veysey, *The Emergence of the American University* (Chicago: University of Chicago Press, 1965).

9. Gerald Grant and David Riesman, *The Perpetual Dream,* pp. 15–18.

10. The decline of general education was caused both by the chang-

ing student market and the indifference of or rejection by the faculty of "general education" courses. Faculties held on to the requirements for the major which they cared about but only to the rhetoric and not to the reality of "general education."

11. Abraham Flexner once wrote that American universities "have thoughtlessly and excessively catered to fleeting, transient, and immediate demands;" *Universities: American, English and German* (New York: Oxford University Press, 1930, 1968), p. 44. This was his central complaint. I, however, take the present situation as a fact, and with some strong arguments for it, as compared with any other system of decision making.

12. "New England's First Fruits, 1643," in Richard Hofstadter and Wilson Smith, eds., *American Higher Education: A Documentary History* (Chicago: University of Chicago Press, 1961), I, 6.

13. For a discussion of the effects of ability and socioeconomic status on enrollment rates in four advanced nations, see Roger L. Geiger, "The Limits of Higher Education: A Comparative Analysis of Factors Affecting Enrollment Levels in Belgium, France, Japan and the United States." Yale Higher Education Research Group Working Paper, YHERG-41, New Haven, Conn., February 1980.

14. "By 1976, the two-hundredth anniversary of the Declaration of Independence, the Commission proposes: That all economic barriers to educational opportunity be eliminated, thus closing the present probability differentials for college access and completion, and graduate school access and completion, among groups of equal academic ability but unequal family income level." The Carnegie Commission on Higher Education, *A Chance to Learn* (New York: McGraw-Hill, 1970), p. 27.

As much as 15 percent of the high-quality talent that might be expected to go on to college does not now do so, based on the short-fall of students in the top quartile in ability from low- and moderate-income families as compared with the attendance rate of students with similar ability from more affluent families. (National Opinion Research Center, Chicago, "High School and Beyond," a study of 1015 U.S. high schools carried out for the National Center for Education Statistics, 1980.)

15. Howard R. Bowen, *Investment in Learning* (San Francisco: Jossey-Bass, 1977); F. Thomas Juster et al., *Education, Income, and Human Behavior* (New York: McGraw-Hill, 1975); Stephen B. Withey, *A Degree and What Else?* (New York: McGraw-Hill, 1971). For a summary of some outcomes of higher education, see Charlotte Alhadeff and Margaret S. Gordon, "Supplement E: Higher Education and Human Performance," in Carnegie Council on Policy Studies in Higher Education, *Three Thousand Futures* (San Francisco: Jossey-Bass, 1980).

16. Daniel Yankelovich, "Work, Values and the New Breed," in Clark Kerr and Jerome Rosow, eds., *Work in America: The Decade Ahead* (New York: Van Nostrand, 1979), p. 10.

17. See Harry Randall Frost, "A Study of Relationships between Certain Characteristics of Statewide Agencies of Higher Education and Selected Indicators of Higher Education," Diss. University of Colorado, 1978.

18. The changes undertaken, which have included much more drastic innovations, have certainly had a substantial impact in some other nations, including Germany, Sweden, Denmark, and the Netherlands.

19. At the beginning of the seventies, forty percent of all students attended colleges and universities which were parts of multicampus institutions. Clark Kerr, "Foreword," in Eugene C. Lee and Frank M. Bowen, *The Multicampus University* (New York: McGraw-Hill, 1971), p. xi.

20. Janet H. Ruyle and Lyman A. Glenny, *State Budgeting for Higher Education: Trends in State Revenue Appropriations from 1968 to 1977* (Berkeley: Center for Studies in Higher Education, University of California, 1978), p. 69.

6. Commentaries on the Golden Age of the Research University

1. In 1969, the American Association of University Professors advised a "maximum teaching load" of nine hours per week and a "preferred teaching load" of six hours "for instruction partly or entirely at the graduate level." American Association of University Professors, *Policy Documents and Reports, 1990*

Edition (Washington, D.C.: American Association of University Professors, 1990), p. 164.

2. See Clark Kerr, *The Great Transformation in Higher Education: 1960–1980* (Albany: State University of New York Press, 1991).

3. Carnegie Commission on Higher Education, *The Purposes and the Performance of Higher Education in the United States* (New York: McGraw-Hill, 1973), Chap. 3, "Purpose 1: The Education of the Individual Student and the Provision of a Constructive Environment for Developmental Growth."

4. *Report of the Commissioners to Inquire into the State, Discipline, Studies and Revenues of the University and Colleges of Oxford, together with the Evidence, and an Appendix.* House of Commons Parliamentary Papers, 1852. Evidence of Mark Pattison, p. 48.

5. Kerr, *The Great Transformation in Higher Education: 1960–1980,* Introduction to Part III, pp. 199–205. Neil Smelser had earlier used the analogy of "estates" in France before the Revolution and their changing comparative situations to explain, with great insight, the rising conflicts within California higher education. See "Growth, Structural Change, and Conflict in California Higher Education, 1950–1970," in Gabriel Almond and Neil Smelser, eds., *Public Higher Education in California* (Berkeley: University of California Press, 1973), pp. 9–142. My use of "estates" was for the purpose of explaining the complexities of internal governance. Eric Ashby in 1970 had still earlier written *The Rise of the Student Estate in Britain* (Cambridge: Harvard University Press, 1970). Ashby has also described the university as a "constellation of anarchies" and a series of "little syndicates." "Ivory Towers in Tomorrow's World," *Journal of Higher Education,* vol. 38, no. 8 (November 1967) pp. 417–427.

6. James B. Conant, Vannevar Bush, and Karl Compton were leading figures in forming the government-university partnership in scientific research during World War II. Their plan for continuing that partnership into the postwar world is outlined in *Science, the Endless Frontier: A Report to the President by Vannevar Bush* (Office of Scientific Research and Development, Washington, D.C.: U.S. Government Printing Office, 1945).

7. Gerald Grant and David Riesman refer to Santa Cruz as "one of the most genuine successes of the last decade," in "Reform and Experiment in the American College," *The Perpetual Dream* (Chicago: University of Chicago Press, 1978), p. 253.

8. James Bryce, *The American Commonwealth,* new edition (New York: Macmillan, 1914), II.

9. Henry Adams, *The Education of Henry Adams* (New York: The Modern Library, 1931 [1918]), pp. 458, 461.

10. Abraham Flexner, *The American College: A Criticism* (New York: Arno Press, 1969 [1908]), pp. 29–30.

11. Immanuel Kant, *The Conflict of the Faculties* (New York: Abaris Books, 1979 [1798]).

12. Henry Rosovsky, "Highest Education," *The New Republic,* July 13 and 20, 1987, pp. 13–14.

13. Robert Heilbroner, *Twenty-First Century Capitalism* (New York: W. W. Norton, 1993), pp. 37 and 145.

14. John F. Hughes, ed., *American Education and the State* (Washington, D.C.: American Council on Education, 1975), 267–275.

15. *Three Thousand Futures* (San Francisco: Jossey-Bass, 1980), p. 13.

16. Letter from T. H. Huxley to E. Ray Lankester, April 11, 1892.

17. See, among others, Carnegie Commission on Higher Education, *Less Time, More Options: Education beyond the High School* (New York: McGraw-Hill, 1971), and *Reform on Campus: Changing Students, Changing Academic Programs* (New York: McGraw-Hill, 1972). See also Clark Kerr, "Rebuilding Communities of Scholars: Toward the More Perfect University," in *The Great Transformation in Higher Education: 1960–1980,* Chap. 22, pp. 285–295. (Originally given as a lecture at a conference in 1967 entitled "The University in America," chaired by Robert Hutchins and sponsored by the Center for the Study of Democratic Institutions. I then looked upon it as my fourth Godkin Lecture, which was never given and which I wished I had given to balance out the presentation.)

18. For a partial listing of some of the many specific attempted internal academic reforms, see Clark Kerr, "Annex: Mutations in Undergraduate Education in the United States—Early 1970s,"

in *Troubled Times for American Higher Education* (Albany: State University of New York Press, 1994), pp. 139–146. This listing was originally presented at a conference in Hiroshima, Japan, in 1976.

19. Robert Paul Wolff, *The Ideal of the University* (New Brunswick: Transaction Publishers, 1992 [1969]), p. 133.

20. Wolff, p. 42.

7. A New Age? From Increasing Federal Riches to Increasing State Poverty

1. Henry Rosovsky, *Dean's Report,* 1990–1991, Faculty of Arts and Sciences (Cambridge: Harvard University).

2. See the discussion in Neil Smelser, "The Politics of Ambivalence," *Dædalus* (Fall 1993); issued as vol. 22, no. 4 of the *Proceedings* of the American Academy of Arts and Sciences), pp. 37–53.

3. See the discussion in John R. Searle, "Rationality and Realism: What Is at Stake?" *Dædalus* (Fall 1993), pp. 55–83.

4. For a discussion of the "passions" and the "interests," see Albert O. Hirschman, *The Passions and the Interests* (Princeton: Princeton University Press, 1977).

5. For a more extended discussion of the second and third characteristics, see Chap. 9, "The Academic Elite and the Professoriate: A 'Disintegrating Profession'?," and Chap. 10, "Academic Citizenship in Decline," in Clark Kerr, *Higher Education Cannot Escape History: Issues for the Twenty-First Century* (Albany: State University of New York Press, 1994).

6. Eric Ashby, "A Hippocratic Oath for the Academic Profession," *Minerva,* vol. 7, nos. 1–2 (Autumn–Winter 1968–1969), pp. 64–66.

7. See the discussion by Zvi Griliches, "Productivity, R&D, and the Data Constraint," *American Economic Review,* vol. 84, no. 1 (March 1994), pp. 1–23.

8. Paul A. Krugman, *The Age of Diminished Expectations* (Cambridge: MIT Press, 1994), p. 9.

9. See the discussion by David Riesman in the introduction to his

1993 edition of *Abundance for What?* (New Brunswick, N.J.: Transaction, 1993), p. xxi.

10. See the discussion in Frank Press, "Science and Technology Policy for the Post–Vannevar Bush Era," in Stephen D. Nelson, Kathleen M. Gramp, and Alfred H. Teich, eds., *AAAS Science and Technology Yearbook, 1992*, Committee on Science, Engineering, and Public Policy for the American Association for the Advancement of Science (Washington, D.C.: American Association for the Advancement of Science, 1993), pp. 3–15.

8. HARD CHOICES

1. See Donald Kennedy, "Making Choices in the Research University," *Dædalus,* Fall 1993 (issued as vol. 122, no. 4 of the *Proceedings* of the American Academy of Arts and Sciences), pp. 127–156.

2. See Kennedy.

3. Carnegie Commission on Higher Education, *Higher Education: Who Pays? Who Benefits? Who Should Pay?* (New York: McGraw-Hill, 1973).

4. Calculated from data in National Science Board, *Science Indicators: 1993* (Washington, D.C.: U.S. Government Printing Office, 1994), Appendix Table 4-3.

5. See the discussion in Robert Heilbroner, *Twenty-First-Century Capitalism* (New York: W. W. Norton, 1993), Chap. 4.

6. Frederick E. Balderston, "Leadership and the Presidency," Chap. 4 of *Managing Today's University: Strategies for Survival, Change, and Excellence,* Second ed. (San Francisco: Jossey-Bass, 1995).

7. Frank Press, "Science and Technology Policy for the post–Vannevar Bush Era," in Stephen D. Nelson, Kathleen M. Gramp, and Alfred H. Teich, eds., *AAAS Science and Technology Yearbook, 1992*, Committee on Science, Engineering, and Public Policy for the American Association for the Advancement of Science (Washington, D.C.: American Association for the Advancement of Science, 1993), pp. 8, 9, 10, 13.

8. Carnegie Commission on Higher Education, *The Fourth Revo-*

lution: Instructional Technology in Higher Education (New York: McGraw-Hill, 1972).

9. Howard R. Bowen, *The State of the Nation and the Agenda for Higher Education* (San Francisco: Jossey-Bass, 1982).

9. THE "CITY OF INTELLECT" IN A CENTURY FOR THE FOXES?

1. This essay was first presented at "The Future of the City of Intellect" Conference at the University of California, Riverside, on February 17, 2000. The conference was organized by Steven Brint, professor of sociology and director of the Center for Ideas and Society, at the University of California, Riverside.

2. See Chapter 3.

3. Ibid., p. 94.

4. David Riesman and Christopher Jencks, *The Academic Revolution* (New York: Doubleday, 1968), p. 17.

5. Henry May, *Ideas, Faith, and Feelings* (New York: Oxford University Press, 1983), p. 96.

6. Eric L. Dey, Alexander W. Astin, and William S. Korn, *The American Freshman: Twenty-Five Year Trends, 1966–1990* (Los Angeles: Higher Education Research Institute, UCLA, 1991).

7. *Science, the Endless Frontier: Report to the President on a Program for Postwar Scientific Research by Vannevar Bush,* (Office of Scientific Research and Development,Washington: U.S. Government Printing Office, 1945).

8. See the discussion in Robert Nisbet, *Teachers & Scholars: A Memoir of Berkeley in Depression and War* (New Brunswick, NJ: Transaction Publishers, 1992), p. 201. Nisbet discusses the shift at Berkeley from a teaching faculty to a research faculty.

9. See p. 78.

10. See Robert Heilbroner, *Visions of the Future: The Distant Past, Yesterday, Today, Tomorrow* (New York: Oxford University Press, 1995).

11. See the discussion in Clark Kerr, *The Gold and the Blue: Academic Triumphs,* vol. I (Berkeley: University of California Press, 2001), Chapter 12.

12. For an excellent discussion of how the IT (information technol-

ogy) revolution is added onto the prior "universal access" revolution and pushes it rapidly forward, and how the United States is advantaged by its history in adapting to both revolutions, see Martin Trow, "From Mass Higher Education to Universal Access: The American Advantage," *Minerva* 37 (Spring 2000), pp. 1–26. See also Martin Trow, "The Development of Information Technology in American Higher Education," *Daedalus,* vol. 126, no. 4 (Fall 1997), pp. 293–314.

13. Isaiah Berlin, *The Hedgehog and The Fox* (New York: Simon & Schuster, 1953).

14. Ibid., pp. 1, 2, 7, 9.

15. Burton R. Clark, *Creating Entrepreneurial Universities: Organizational Pathways of Transformation* (Oxford: International Association of Universities and Elsevier Science Ltd./Pergamon, 1998).

16. Michael Shattock, "The Internal and External Threats to the University of the Twenty-First Century," *Minerva* 30 (Summer 1992), p. 146.

17. Ernest Boyer and Fred M. Hechinger, *Higher Learning in the Nation's Service* (Washington: Carnegie Foundation for the Advancement of Teaching, 1981), p. 3.

18. Peter F. Drucker, "The Next Information Revolution," *Forbes ASAP* (August 14, 1998).

19. Drucker said: "I consider the American research university of the last 40 years to be a failure." (Peter F. Drucker, teleconference address quoted in Dennis Normile, "Schools Ponder New Global Landscape," *Science,* vol. 277, no. 5324 [July 18, 1997], p. 311.)

20. Arthur Levine, "The Soul of A New University," *New York Times* (March 13, 2000), p. A21.

21. Unpublished manuscript.

22. Henry J. Aaron and Robert D. Reischauer, "Will the Baby Boomers Break the Bank?" in Richard C. Leone and Greg Anrig, Jr., eds., *Social Security: Beyond the Basics* (New York: The Century Foundation Press, 1999), p. 52.

23. Peter Schrag, *Paradise Lost: California's Experience and America's Future* (New York: New Press, 1998), Part Four.

24. Derek Bok, *The Cost of Talent: How Executives and Professionals Are Paid and How It Affects America* (New York: Free Press, 1993).
25. John R. Searle, "Rationality and Realism, What is at Stake?" *Daedalus*, vol. 122, no. 4 (Fall 1993), p. 56.
26. Clark Kerr, testimony before the Joint Committee to Develop a Master Plan for Education, Kindergarten through University (Senator Dede Alpert, Chair), The California Legislature, Sacramento, California, August 24, 1999.
27. See Chapter 5.
28. For early efforts in this direction, see Malcolm S. M. Watts and Clark Jones, *The Story of the California AHEC System: California Area Health Education Centers: 1972–1989* (Fresno: California AHEC System, 1990); Charles Odegaard, *Eleven Area Health Education Centers: The View from the Grass Roots* (Berkeley: Carnegie Council on Policy Studies in Higher Education, 1980); and Carnegie Commission on Higher Education, *Higher Education and the Nation's Health: Policies for Medical and Dental Education* (New York: McGraw-Hill, 1970).
29. Henry Rosovsky, *The University: an Owner's Manual* (New York: W. W. Norton, 1990).
30. Howard R. Bowen, *The State of the Nation and the Agenda for Higher Education* (San Francisco: Jossey-Bass, 1982).
31. Howard R. Bowen, *Investment in Learning* (San Francisco: Jossey-Bass, 1977).

INDEX